THOMAS TRAHERNE

THE SELECTED WRITINGS OF
THOMAS TRAHERNE

edited by Dick Davis

FYFIELD BOOKS
Carcanet   Manchester

First published 1980 by
Carcanet New Press Limited
330 Corn Exchange Buildings
Manchester M4 3BG

Printed in England by Billings, Guildford

CONTENTS

INTRODUCTION

WHEN Traherne's poems were discovered in 1896 (on a London bookstall) the unsigned manuscript was at first ascribed to Henry Vaughan. But the literary scholar Bertram Dobell was struck by a similarity between the diction of the poems and that of passages in an obscure book of religious meditations, *A Serious and Pathetical Contemplation of the Mercies of God, in Several most Devout and Sublime Thanksgivings for the Same*, which had been published in 1699. The anonymous author of the book's preface claimed that the 'Thanksgivings' had been written by Thomas Traherne, who had died twenty-five years previously in 1674. Dobell became convinced that the author of the new 'Vaughan' manuscript and that of the *Thanksgivings* were one and the same man: his intuition was supported by research, further manuscripts came to light, and with the publication of Traherne's poems (in 1903 and 1910) a new seventeenth century poet of remarkable intensity and limpidity took his place in the history of English verse.

Well, almost. Sadly, that first ascription to Vaughan has dogged Traherne ever since, and he is often considered merely as a kind of decadent and laxer version of the older poet. It is true that Vaughan's influence on him is palpable: Part I of Vaughan's *Silex Scintillans* was published in 1650, when Traherne was thirteen years old, and not only one of Vaughan's chief subjects (the felicity of childhood) but his very verse forms are recognizable in Traherne's work. But Vaughan is, in fact, closer to his master, George Herbert, than he is to his disciple Traherne. If *Silex Scintillans* was a starting point for Traherne, his poems are far from being imitations of Vaughan and to consider them as such is to judge them by a standard alien to their nature. There is a propriety, a kind of just tact of sentiment, and a seamlessness of thought and form about most of Vaughan's verse which is strongly reminiscent of Herbert, but which Traherne never attempts. Here is Vaughan:

> Lord! what a busy, restless thing
> Hast thou made man!
> Each day and hour he is on wing,
> Rests not a span.

And here is Traherne expressing the same idea:

> No walls confine! Can nothing hold my mind?
> Can I no rest nor satisfaction find?
> Must I behold eternity
> And see
> What things above the heavens be?

Both begin with exclamations, but Vaughan's lines are a grammatical and comparatively sober statement of his theme: Traherne's exclamation is cut short (what is the object of 'confine'?—obviously 'my mind', but the poet's precipitate haste leaves us to supply it for ourselves) and immediately dissolves in unanswered questions. The verse looks constantly and impatiently forward, it seems to worry its subject like an excited animal giving chase, whereas Vaughan's statement rests comfortably in its chosen form. And most important, as the remainder of these two poems makes plain, Traherne *approves* of this 'insatiableness', he takes it as proof of his soul's desire for infinity and therefore for God, whereas Vaughan sees it as the prelude to rest. Vaughan's poem ends with an image of cradled safety, the sick soul nursed by God, its restlessness put by; whereas Traherne's poem seeks a kind of dissolving of the mind in infinity, an ecstatic vision of and participation in eternity. Further, Vaughan's meaning is much more detachable than Traherne's: Traherne's poem does not resolve into a 'moral', a gnomic summing up, as Vaughan's does (very much in the manner of Herbert); it merely stops.

Traherne is doing something very different with form from either Herbert or Vaughan. And because these two poets are his obvious predecessors he has been judged by their standards and found wanting. The complexity of Herbert's stanza forms is used to give a sense of justice and balance, of the mind returning to an old way with a new insight, of difficulties posed and resolved, so that the reader has been led through an argument or a series of states of mind by the time he reaches the end of the poem; and the final resolution of the argument, the final state of mind in which the poem rests, is felt to be just, a more mature or more wise understanding of the nature of things than is shown at the poem's opening. It is a poetry of reconciliation to what Herbert took to be the facts of his life, and it is this almost 'pat' acceptance that gives a few of his poems a tinge of complacency. Vaughan's poems too move towards understanding —a difficulty is posed and resolved, the moral is drawn. The poems seek equilibrium, even if they do not begin with it. But Traherne's poems are a nervous, restless flight. We have only to compare their relative techniques to see this. Herbert's poems are typically built on an allegory—a piece of church furniture is used as a symbol of some facet of man's spiritual life, and the poem continually returns to the underlying metaphor. Traherne almost never proceeds in this way, and his poetry never comes to rest in a familiar, tangible object as does Herbert's. His typical words are abstract—or so intangible as to seem abstract—eternity, light, mind, soul, day, sky. This intangible vocabulary gives the poems immense airiness, a feeling of plunging through space and of not knowing quite where one is. When he does mention familiar objects they are very often given to us pell-mell in a list, and their appearance, far from stabilizing the poem in quotidian reality, gives it a further air of headlong precipitancy, as if the mind can rest in no single object but moves on immediately to another and then another. The mind in his poems seems to tremble at the brink of ineffable discovery, to be about to dissolve into another mode of being. In his poem 'On News' he describes the soul straining to be free of the body and in 'Shadows in the Water' and 'On Leaping over the Moon' the world the child sees reflected in water is not merely an image of our reality but another world entirely to which the child feels he shall, 'when that thin skin/Is broken, be admitted in'. It is this sense of imminent revelation, or of imminent entrance into an inheritance already perceived, that gives his poems their remarkably individual tone.

The basic strategy for communicating meaning in Herbert's poems is the extended metaphor: this is rarely employed by Traherne, indeed in his opening poem, 'The Author to the Critical Peruser', he rejects metaphor as a way of proceeding. Rather his favourite devices are lists, rhetorical questions, apostrophes—all rhetorical gestures that lead the reader further in, and that, rather than offering resolution, deny it. The ends of Herbert's and Vaughan's poems often contain their most moving lines; the reader is as it were led home (and even tucked up in bed!) by the poet; but the ends of Traherne's poems are curiously 'open' and unexpected—simply because there is no natural end, no resolution towards which the poem is moving. His finest closing passage is probably the last stanza of 'Solitude', and this is because in this poem the lack of resolution is the point, it is what the poem is about. More usually there is a final, frustrated flourish—a kind of sigh that language cannot go further. The reader has not been led home but is launched into emptiness and is suddenly left to fend for himself.

Herbert almost never repeats a stanza form and neither does Traherne, but whereas this has been taken as evidence of Herbert's technical virtuosity it has been mentioned in Traherne's case as a reproach. Anne Ridler, in her introduction to the Oxford edition of his poems, has written, 'the fact that he never repeated a stanza pattern meant that he never became entirely at ease with any'. It seems unjust to castigate one poet for what is seen as a virtue in another, and yet Herbert does seem at home in his forms, whereas Traherne seems to attempt to fly their limitations. But it is Traherne's very use of form that enables him to convey this sense of perpetually being about to overcome exigencies of rhyme and metre and speak to us in some wholly unbodied way. His apparent disdain for form is achieved almost wholly by formal means, and this paradox has led his formal excellence to be underrated.

His frequent elisions (e.g. almost all words that contain a 'v' between two vowels are elided, so that 'even' is pronounced 'e'en' and 'heaven' nine times out of ten as 'heav'n') and the constant use of run-over lines go part of the way to explaining that sense of nervous impatience that is so characteristic of the movement of his verse. And the different line-lengths, that in Herbert seem to echo and support one another like symmetrical features of a labyrinthine building, in Traherne's work seem like paradigms of the hesitancy and sudden confidences of his mental restlessness.

That this impression of spontaneous mental activity was worked for is easily proved if we examine the masterly internal rhymes of 'Solitude'. In this poem the last two lines of each stanza contain internal rhymes, generally the third or fourth syllable rhyming with the seventh or eighth. (This is not true of the third stanza, but I suspect this is due to a 'correction' by Traherne's brother Philip, who perhaps had not noticed this recurrent pattern.) These rhymes add immeasurably to the emphatic quality of each stanza's concluding statement, yet they are so masterfully integrated into the flow of the poem that I would guess their presence is unnoticed by most readers. Such dexterity does not come easily, and it is ironic that Traherne's very skill in giving the impression of spontaneity should be the cause of the accusation that he lacks technical skill. At his best he is a master of form, fully the equal of Herbert or Vaughan: we have been deceived by the fact that the ends to which he uses form are so different from the ends of his predecessors, while the forms themselves seem superficially to be similar. He does not attempt the lapidary or the gnomic, where form is symmetrical and supportive. His echoes do not turn back and confirm but lead on, breathlessly. This impatience is conveyed in great part by an astonishing mastery of rhythm, a mastery so great that it seems entirely inborn, as in the greatest musicians; so that we consider his successes lucky hits and his failures evidence of poor control. But his successes are the product of a very impressive technical facility. It is true that his work is uneven, and we can read a poem of his with which we are not familiar with a tense expectation of imminent failure, so breathtaking are his leaps and flights. But a poet deserves to be judged by his best work, and Traherne's best—as in 'Solitude', 'On News', 'Shadows in the Water', 'Wonder', and 'The Apostasy'—is uniquely moving and accomplished.

In the same way that his rhythms can seem sprawling until one realizes what he is trying to do with them, so he can appear naive and unsophisticated when compared to other seventeenth-century religious poets. But the 'naivety', like the 'spontaneous' rhythms, has been chosen. He was a graduate of Brasenose College, Oxford, and a Bachelor of Divinity; some of his poems (e.g. 'My Spirit') show a probable acquaintance with the writings of the Cambridge Platonists: the only work of his published in his lifetime, *Roman Forgeries*, was an examination of the authenticity or otherwise of the Donation of Constantine and other documents related to Catholicism. He certainly was not a naive, self-taught enthusiast, but for his time a relatively learned man, learned particularly in the history of the church and in philosophy. (The 'Fourth Century' is largely a defence of philosophy, and its tone is highly personal, as if Traherne had been accused of preferring philosophy to faith and were defending himself accordingly.)

What kind of man was he? He was born in Herefordshire in 1637, the son of a shoe-maker who died when Thomas and his brother Philip were quite young. He was then apparently brought up by his paternal uncle, who was an altogether more successful man than his father, having been twice mayor of Hereford. (Traherne mentions the mayor's gown in 'Solitude'.) It was probably this uncle who paid for his university education, but Traherne never forgot the poverty of his earliest years, and it is hinted at both in the *Centuries* and in several poems. In 1661 he became the parish priest of Credenhill, near Hereford, and here he made the acquaintance of Susanna Hopton, whose spiritual adviser he became. In 1669 he became chaplain to Sir Orlando Bridgeman, and this involved his removal to London and Teddington. It was this absence from Susanna Hopton that seems to have prompted him to write for her edification his most important—and unfinished—prose work, the *Centuries of Meditation*. He died relatively young in 1674.

The preface to the 1699 edition of his *Thanksgivings*—the book that led Dobell to suspect the newly found poems were Traherne's and not Vaughan's—is thought to have been written by Susanna Hopton. Certainly the passages describing Traherne fit well with the image of the man which we derive from his writings. He is said to have been:

so wonderfully transported with the love of God to mankind, with the excellency of those divine laws which are prescribed to us, and with those inexpressible felicities to which we are entitled by being created in, and redeemed to, the Divine Image; that he dwelt continually amongst these thoughts, with great delight and satisfaction, spending most of his time when at home in digesting his notion of these things into writing, and was so full of them when abroad that those that would converse with him were forced to endure some discourse upon these subjects, whether they had any sense of religion or not.

And later the preface continues:

He was a man of a cheerful and sprightly temper, free from any-thing of the sourness or formality by which some great pretenders of piety rather disparage and misrepresent true religion than recommend it; and therefore was very affable and pleasant in his conversation, ready to do all good offices to his friends and chari-table to the poor almost beyond his ability. But being removed

out of the country to the service of the late Lord Keeper Bridgeman, as his chaplain, he died young, and got early to those
blissful mansions to which he at all times aspired.

Traherne is perhaps best remembered for his descriptions of the innocent wonder of his childhood, and his insistence on the value of these
experiences, not only in themselves but as a guide to adult life. Such
sentiments are familiar to us from a great deal of nineteenth-century
poetry, and when we read Traherne we often forget how very peculiar
(in both senses) they must have been in the seventeenth century. We
read him with the writings of Blake and Wordsworth (and even
Rousseau) intervening, and in doing so we subtly misrepresent him to
ourselves. Traherne's wonder appears to him in a specifically religious
guise, as evidence of the beneficence of God and of his own nearness to
God. It does not have the social implications of Blake (who emphasizes
the child's helpless innocence as a reproach to the society that
represses or exploits it) nor the nature-worshipping implications of
Wordsworth. Traherne almost never mentions by name an item of
flora or fauna—there are flowers in his poems but no violets or daff-
odils. Nature for him is evidence of the glory of God only when it is
'esteemed' (one of his favourite words) correctly, and its particulars
as things in themselves do not interest him. What interests him is his
vision, not what his vision illuminates, and his vision as evidence of
his blessed, unfallen state.

Where do these ideas come from? The obvious source is again
Vaughan, though Traherne is altogether more emphatic in his claims,
and whatever external source there may have been for his beliefs
must have been augmented by overwhelming personal conviction.
Vaughan's ideas perhaps came from his brother who was well-known
in the seventeenth century for his study of esoteric philosophies. Both
poets probably owe a great deal to the Cambridge Platonists, in parti-
cular the idea of the pre-existence of the human soul, at which they
hint; but it is probably easiest to see them, especially the more ex-
uberant Traherne, as representatives of that recurrent English/Celtic
heresy, Pelagianism.

Pelagius was a British monk of the fourth and fifth centuries; 'his
name in Welsh was Morgan, which signifies the sea'. He denied the
doctrine of original sin, asserting that Adam's fall did not involve

his posterity. His doctrines were condemned by Pope Zosimus in 418. Traherne must have been aware, as a student of the history of the church, that these opinions were heretical, and he does try at some points to accommodate his beliefs to orthodoxy, but he soon gives up the unequal attempt (e.g. 'Third Century', Section 8, in which he only admits that Adam set a very bad example by his fall, which is quite different from the orthodox view that his fall automatically involved the whole of subsequent humanity). For Traherne man is born 'an empty book . . . in which anything may be written' ('First Century', Section 1); his fall is personal, and is the result of 'custom' which leads him astray. By rejecting custom he can regain his original purity. The seventeenth century was probably the first time for many hundreds of years that a man could have held such beliefs without incurring martyrdom or at the least official censure.

Like Wordsworth Traherne suffered a diminution of his original intensity of vision, and many of the most moving passages of the *Centuries* (particularly from the autobiographical 'Third Century') and one of his finest poems, 'Solitude', deal with this sense of loss. But unlike Wordsworth he thought the lost vision recoverable, and claims to have recovered it. For Wordsworth the diminution was an unavoidable aspect of the human condition, the sheer fact of growing older made it inevitable. But for Traherne the loss is the result of a rectifiable mistake, that of valuing 'custom', the man-made world, instead of God's or the natural world. Traherne specifically says that when he made this discovery the vision was restored to him ('Third Century', Section 46) and it is wrong to think of him, as we think of certain Romantic poets, as spending his adult life mourning the lost purity of childhood. For Traherne childhood was merely the time before he had made the mistake of valuing 'custom', and it was not therefore intrinsically superior to adulthood. When he admonishes Susanna Hopton to remember the innocence of infancy, this is only because he believed that at this time people 'esteemed' the world 'aright', being as yet uncorrupted. The vision was recoverable; and that note of elegiac pathos, mourning irretrievably lost innocence, so dear to the Romantics, is absent from Traherne.

14

A NOTE ON THE TEXT

There is a problem about the manuscripts of Traherne's poems. Some of them exist in two copies—one by the author and one by his brother Philip (who seems to have prepared them for publication). Some exist only in copies by Philip. When there are two copies available we can see that Philip made frequent minor corrections in his brother's poems—mostly of a tidying-up nature—and that these corrections are nearly always unfortunate. It is not only that we should in any case prefer the author's version, even if it were worse, but that Thomas's original is actually better. It is therefore virtually certain that those poems which survive only in Philip's copies have been slightly doctored. In this selection the poems up to and including 'On News' (p. 46) are ones of which we have both brothers' versions, and the one given here is Thomas's original. After this point are the poems that exist only in Philip's transcriptions, except for the last two poems, which again are given in Thomas's version.

The spelling has been modernized throughout. Both brothers punctuated their manuscripts very heavily, and the punctuation has been brought more into line with modern usage, though I have sometimes left Traherne's riot of exclamation marks as in the original, as they seem part of the poems' overall tone.

D.D.

THE AUTHOR TO THE CRITICAL PERUSER

The naked truth in many faces shown,
Whose inward beauties very few have known,
A simple light, transparent words, a strain
That lowly creeps, yet maketh mountains plain,
Brings down the highest mysteries to sense
And keeps them there—that is our excellence,
At that we aim; to th' end thy soul might see
With open eyes thy great felicity,
Its objects view, and trace the glorious way
Whereby thou may'st thy highest bliss enjoy.

No curling metaphors that gild the sense,
Nor pictures here, nor painted eloquence;
No florid streams of superficial gems,
But real crowns and thrones and diadems!
That gold on gold should hiding shining lie
May well be reckoned baser heraldry.

An easy style drawn from a native vein,
A clearer stream than that which poets feign,
Whose bottom may, how deep so-e'er, be seen,
Is that which I think fit to win esteem:
Else we could speak *Zamzummim* words, and tell
A tale in tongues that sound like Babel-Hell;
In meteors speak, in blazing prodigies,
Things that amaze, but will not make us wise.

On shining banks we could nigh Tagus walk;
In flowery meads of rich Pactolus talk;
Bring in the druids, and the Sibyls view;
See what the rites are which the Indians do;
Derive along the channel of our quill
The streams that flow from high Parnassus' hill;
Ransack all nature's rooms, and add the things
Which Persian courts enrich, to make us kings:

To make us kings indeed! Not verbal ones,
But real kings, exalted unto thrones,
And more than golden thrones! 'Tis this I do,
Letting poetic strains and shadows go.

I cannot imitate their vulgar sense
Who clothes admire, not the man they fence
Against the cold; and while they wonder at
His rings, his precious stones, his gold and plate—
The middle piece, his body and his mind,
They overlook, no beauty in them find.
God's works they slight, their own they magnify,
His they condemn, or careless pass them by.

Their woven silks and well-made suits they prize,
Value their gems, but not their useful eyes:
Their precious hands, their tongues and lips divine,
Their polished flesh where whitest lilies join
With blushing roses and with sapphire veins,
The bones, the joints, and that which else remains
Within that curious fabric, life and strength,
In the well-compacted breadth and depth and length
Of various limbs, that living engines be
Of glorious worth, God's work they will not see:
Nor yet the soul, in whose concealèd face,
Which comprehendeth all unbounded space,
God may be seen; though she can understand
The length of ages and the tracts of land
That from the zodiac do extended lie
Unto the poles, and view eternity.

Even thus do idle fancies, toys and words,
(Like gilded scabbards hiding rusty swords)
Take vulgar souls, who gaze on rich attire
But God's diviner works do ne'er admire.

THE SALUTATION

These little limbs,
　These eyes and hands which here I find,
These rosy cheeks wherewith my life begins,
　Where have ye been? Behind
What curtain were ye from me hid so long?
Where was, in what abyss, my speaking tongue?

　When silent I
　So many thousand, thousand years,
Beneath the dust did in a chaos lie,
　How could I smiles or tears,
Or lips or hands or eyes or ears perceive?
Welcome ye treasures which I now receive.

　I that so long
　Was nothing from eternity,
Did little think such joys as ear or tongue
　To celebrate or see;
Such sounds to hear, such hands to feel, such feet,
Beneath the skies, on such a ground to meet.

　New burnished joys!
　Which yellow gold and pearl excel!
Such sacred treasures are the limbs in boys
　In which a soul doth dwell:
Their organizèd joints and azure veins
More wealth include than all the world contains.

　From dust I rise
　And out of nothing now awake,
These brighter regions which salute mine eyes
　A gift from God I take.
The earth, the seas, the light, the day, the skies,
The sun and stars are mine, if those I prize.

Long time before
I in my mother's womb was born,
A God preparing did this glorious store,
The world, for me adorn.
Into this Eden so divine and fair,
So wide and bright, I come His son and heir.

A stranger here
Strange things doth meet, strange glories see;
Strange treasures lodged in this fair world appear,
Strange all, and new to me.
But that they mine should be, who nothing was,
That strangest is of all, yet brought to pass.

WONDER

How like an angel came I down!
How bright are all things here!
When first among His works I did appear
O how their glory did me crown!
The world resembled His eternity,
In which my soul did walk;
And everything that I did see
Did with me talk.

The skies in their magnificence,
The lively, lovely air;
O how divine, how soft, how sweet, how fair!
The stars did entertain my sense,
And all the works of God so bright and pure,
So rich and great did seem,
As if they ever must endure
In my esteem.

A native health and innocence
Within my bones did grow,

And while my God did all his glories show
    I felt a vigour in my sense
That was all spirit. I within did flow
      With seas of life like wine;
  I nothing in the world did know
        But 'twas divine.

Harsh, ragged objects were concealed
      Oppressions, tears and cries,
Sins, griefs, complaints, dissensions, weeping eyes
    Were hid, and only things revealed
Which heavenly spirits and the angels prize.
      The state of innocence
    And bliss, not trades and poverties,
        Did fill my sense.

The streets were paved with golden stones
      The boys and girls were mine,
Oh how did all their lovely faces shine!
    The sons of men were holy ones.
Joy, beauty, welfare did appear to me,
      And everything which here I found
    While like an angel I did see
        Adorned the ground.

Rich diamond and pearl and gold
      In every place was seen;
Rare splendours—yellow, blue, red, white and green,
    Mine eyes did everywhere behold,
Great wonders clothed with glory did appear,
      Amazement was my bliss:
    That and my wealth was everywhere,
        No joy to this!

Cursed and devised proprieties,
      With envy, avarice
And fraud, those fiends that spoil even Paradise,

Fled from the splendour of mine eyes.
And so did hedges, ditches, limits, bounds,
 I dreamed not aught of those,
 But wandered over all men's grounds,
  And found repose.

Proprieties themselves were mine,
  And hedges ornaments;
Walls, boxes, coffers and their rich contents
 Did not divide my joys but shine.
Clothes, ribbons, jewels, laces, I esteemed
  My joys by others worn;
 For me they all to wear them seemed
  When I was born.

EDEN

A learnèd and a happy ignorance
  Divided me
 From all the vanity,
From all the sloth, care, pain and sorrow that advance
 The madness and the misery
Of men. No error, no distraction I
Saw soil the earth or overcloud the sky.

I knew not that there was a serpent's sting,
  Whose poison shed
  On men did overspread
The world; nor did I dream of such a thing
 As sin, in which mankind lay dead.
They all were brisk and living wights to me,
Yea pure, and full of immortality.

Joy, pleasure, beauty, kindness, glory, love
  Sleep, day, life, light,
  Peace, melody, my sight,

My ears and heart did fill, and freely move.
    All that I saw did me delight.
The universe was then a world of treasure,
To me an universal world of pleasure.

Unwelcome penitence was then unknown,
          Vain, costly toys,
        Swearing and roaring boys,
Shops, markets, taverns, coaches were unshown;
     So all things were that drowned my joys.
No briars choked up my path, nor hid the face
Of bliss and beauty, nor eclipsed the place.

Only what Adam in his first estate
        Did I behold;
      Hard silver and dry gold
As yet lay underground; my blessèd fate
    Was more acquainted with the old
And innocent delights which he did see
In his original simplicity.

Those things which first his Eden did adorn
        My infancy
      Did crown. Simplicity
Was my protection when I first was born.
    Mine eyes those treasures first did see
Which God first made. The first effects of love
My first enjoyments upon earth did prove,

And were so great, and so divine, so pure,
        So fair and sweet,
      So true, when I did meet
Them here at first, they did my soul allure
    And drew away my infant feet
Quite from the works of men, that I might see
The glorious wonders of the Deity.

INNOCENCE

1

But that which most I wonder at, which most
I did esteem my bliss, which most I boast
And ever shall enjoy, is that within
    I felt no stain nor spot of sin.

    No darkness then did overshade,
    But all within was pure and bright,
    No guilt did crush nor fear invade,
    But all my soul was full of light.

    A joyful sense and purity
        Is all I can remember.
    The very night to me was bright,
    'Twas summer in December.

2

A serious meditation did employ
My soul within, which, taken up with joy,
Did seem no outward thing to note, but fly
    All objects that do feed the eye.

    While it those very objects did
    Admire, and prize, and praise, and love,
    Which in their glory most are hid,
    Which presence only doth remove.

    Their constant daily presence I
        Rejoicing at did see—
    And that which takes them from the eye
    Of others offered them to me.

3

No inward inclination did I feel
To avarice or pride; my soul did kneel

In admiration all the day. No lust nor strife
　　Polluted then my infant life.

　　No fraud nor anger in me moved,
　　No malice, jealousy or spite;
　　All that I saw I truly loved.
　　Contentment only and delight

　　Were in my soul. O heaven! what bliss
　　　　Did I enjoy and feel!
　　What powerful delight did this
　　Inspire! for this I daily kneel.

4

Whether it be that nature is so pure
And custom only vicious, or that sure
God did by miracle the guilt remove
　　And make my soul to feel his love

　　So early; or that 'twas one day
　　Where in this happiness I found,
　　Whose strength and brightness so do ray
　　That still it seemeth to surround:

　　What e'er it is, it is a light
　　　　So endless unto me
　　That I a world of true delight
　　Did then and to this day do see.

5

That prospect was the gate of heaven, that day
The ancient light of Eden did convey
Into my soul: I was an Adam there,
　　A little Adam in a sphere

　　Of joys! O there my ravished sense
　　Was entertained in paradise

And had a sight of innocence.
All was beyond all bound and price.

An antepast of heaven sure!
    I on the earth did reign;
Within, without me, all was pure:
I must become a child again.

THE PREPARATIVE

My body being dead, my limbs unknown,
    Before I skilled to prize
    Those living stars mine eyes,
Before my tongue or cheeks were to me shown,
    Before I knew my hands were mine,
Or that my sinews did my members join,
    When neither nostril, foot, nor ear
As yet was seen, or felt, or did appear;
        I was within
A house I knew not, newly clothed with skin.

Then was my soul my only all to me,
    A living, endless eye
    Far wider than the sky
Whose power, whose act, whose essence was to see.
    I was an inward sphere of light,
Or an interminable orb of sight,
    An endless and a living day,
A vital sun that round about did ray
      All life and sense,
A naked, simple, pure intelligence.

I then no thirst nor hunger did conceive,
    No dull necessity,
    No want was known to me;
Without disturbance then I did receive

The fair ideas of all things,
And had the honey even without the stings.
    A meditating, inward eye
Gazing at quiet did within me lie,
        And every thing
Delighted me that was their heavenly king.

For sight inherits beauty, hearing sounds,
        The nostril sweet perfumes,
        All tastes have hidden rooms
Within the tongue, and feeling feeling wounds
    With pleasure and delight, but I
Forgot the rest, and was all sight or eye;
    Unbodied and devoid of care,
Just as in heaven the holy angels are.
        For simple sense
Is lord of all created excellence.

Being thus prepared for all felicity,
        Not prepossessed with dross,
        Nor stiffly glued to gross
And dull materials that might ruin me,
    Not fettered by an iron fate
With vain affections in my earthly state
    To any thing that might seduce
My sense, or else bereave it of its use
        I was as free
As if there were nor sin, nor misery.

Pure empty powers that did nothing loathe
        Did like the fairest glass
        Or spotless, polished brass
Themselves soon in their objects' image clothe.
    Divine impressions when they came
Did quickly enter and my soul inflame.
    'Tis not the object, but the light
That maketh heaven; 'tis a purer sight.

Felicity
Appears to none but them that purely see.

A disentangled and a naked sense,
    A mind that's unpossessed,
    A disengagèd breast,
An empty and a quick intelligence
    Acquainted with the golden mean,
An even spirit, pure and serene,
    Is that where beauty, excellence
And pleasure keep their court of residence.
    My soul retire,
Get free, and so thou shalt even all admire.

DUMBNESS

Sure man was born to meditate on things,
And to contemplate the eternal springs
Of God and nature, glory, bliss and pleasure,
That life and love might be his heavenly treasure:
And therefore speechless made at first, that he
Might in himself profoundly busied be,
And not vent out before he hath ta'en in
Those antidotes that guard his soul from sin.

Wise nature made him deaf too, that he might
Not be disturbed while he doth take delight
In inward things, nor be depraved with tongues,
Nor injured by the errors and the wrongs
That mortal words convey. For sin and death
Are most infusèd by accursèd breath
That flowing from corrupted entrails bear
Those hidden plagues that souls alone may fear.

This, my dear friends, this was my blessèd case;
For nothing spoke to me but the fair face

Of heaven and earth, before my self could speak—
I then my bliss did, when my silence, break.
My non-intelligence of human words
Ten thousand pleasures unto me affords;
For while I knew not what they to me said,
Before their souls were into mine conveyed,
Before that living vehicle of wind
Could breathe into me their infected mind,
Before my thoughts were leavened with theirs, before
There any mixture was; the holy door
Or gate of souls was closed, and mine being one
Within itself to me alone was known.
Then did I dwell within a world of light,
Distinct and separate from all men's sight,
Where I did feel strange thoughts, and secrets see
That were, or seemed, only revealed to me—
There I saw all the world enjoyed by one,
There I was in the world my self alone;
No business serious seemed but one; no work
But one was found, and that did in me lurk.
   D'ye ask me what? It was with clearer eyes
To see all creatures full of deities,
Especially oneself, and to admire
The satisfaction of all true desire;
'Twas to be pleased with all that God hath done,
'Twas to enjoy even all beneath the sun,
'Twas with a steady and immediate sense
To feel and measure all the excellence
Of things; 'Twas to inherit endless treasure
And to be filled with everlasting pleasure;
To reign in silence, and to sing alone,
To see, love, covet, have, enjoy and praise in one;
To prize and to be ravished; to be true,
Sincere and single in a blessèd view
Of all His gifts. Thus was I pent within
A fort, impregnable to any sin,
Till the avenues being open laid,

Whole legions entered and the forts betrayed.
Before which time a pulpit in my mind,
A temple and a teacher I did find,
With a large text to comment on. No ear
But eyes themselves were all the hearers there.
But every stone, and every star a tongue,
And every gale of wind a curious song.
The heavens were an oracle and spake
Divinity; the earth did undertake
The office of a priest, and I being dumb
(Nothing besides was dumb) all things did come
With voices and instructions; but when I
Had gained a tongue their power began to die.
Mine ears let other noises in, not theirs,
A noise disturbing all my songs and prayers.
My foes pulled down the temple to the ground,
They my adoring soul did deeply wound,
And casting that into a swoon destroyed
The oracle, and all I there enjoyed.
And having once inspired me with a sense
Of foreign vanities they march out thence
In troops that cover and despoil my coasts,
Being the invisible, most hurtful hosts.

Yet the first words mine infancy did hear,
The things which in my dumbness did appear,
Preventing all the rest, got such a root
Within my heart, and stick so close unto't,
It may be trampled on but still will grow,
And nutriment to soil itself will owe.
The first impressions are immortal all;
And let mine enemies hoop, cry, roar, call,
Yet these will whisper if I will but hear,
And penetrate the heart if not the ear.

A quiet, silent person may possess
All that is great or high in blessedness.
The inward work is the supreme, for all
The other were occasioned by the fall.
A man that seemeth idle to the view
Of others may the greatest business do.
Those acts which Adam in his innocence
Performed carry all the excellence.
These outward, busy acts he knew not were
But meaner matters, of a lower sphere.
Building of churches, giving to the poor,
In dust and ashes lying on the floor,
Administering of justice, preaching peace,
Ploughing and toiling for a forced increase,
With visiting the sick, or governing
The rude and ignorant—this was a thing
As then unknown. For neither ignorance
Nor poverty, nor sickness did advance
Their banner in the world till sin came in:
These therefore were occasioned all by sin.
The first and only work he had to do
Was in himself to feel his bliss, to view
His sacred treasures, to admire, rejoice,
Sing praises with a sweet and heavenly voice,
See, prize, give thanks within, and love
(Which is the high and only work, above
Them all). And this at first was mine; these were
My exercises of the highest sphere.
To see, approve, take pleasure and rejoice
Within is better than an empty voice,
No melody in words can equal that,
The sweetest organ, lute or harp is flat
And dull compared thereto. And O, that still
I might admire my Father's love and skill!
This is to honour, worship and adore,

This is to love Him: nay it is far more,
It is to enjoy Him and to imitate
The life and glory of His high estate.
'Tis to receive with holy reverence,
To understand His gifts, and with a sense
Of pure devotion and humility
To prize His works, His love to magnify.
O happy ignorance of other things
Which made me present with the King of kings!
And like Him too! All spirit, life and power,
All love and joy, in His eternal bower.
A world of innocence as then was mine
In which the joys of paradise did shine,
And while I was not here I was in heaven
Not resting one but every day in seven,
Forever minding with a lively sense
The universe in all its excellence.
No other thoughts did intervene to cloy,
Divert, extinguish or eclipse my joy.
No other customs, new-found wants or dreams
Invented here polluted my pure streams.
No aloes or dregs, no wormwood star
Was seen to fall into the sea from far.
No rotten soul did like an apple near
My soul approach. There's no contagion here.
An unperceivèd donor gave all pleasures,
There nothing was but I and all my treasures.
In that fair world one only was the friend,
One golden stream, one spring, one only end.
There only one did sacrifice and sing
To only one eternal heavenly king.
The union was so strait between them two
That all was either's which my soul could view.
His gifts and my possessions, both our treasures,
He mine, and I the ocean of His pleasures.
He was an ocean of delights from whom
The living springs and golden streams did come,

My bosom was an ocean into which
They all did run. And me they did enrich.
A vast and infinite capacity
Did make my bosom like the Deity,
In whose mysterious and celestial mind
All ages and all worlds together shined,
Who though He nothing said did always reign
And in Himself eternity contain.
The world was more in me than I in it.
The king of glory in my soul did sit,
And to Himself in me He always gave
All that He takes delight to see me have.
For so my spirit was an endless sphere
Like God Himself, and heaven and earth was there.

MY SPIRIT

My naked, simple life was I.
    That act so strongly shined
  Upon the earth, the sea, the sky,
It was the substance of my mind,
    The sense itself was I.
I felt no dross nor matter in my soul,
No brims nor borders such as in a bowl
We see; my essence was capacity
    That felt all things,
    The thought that springs
Therefrom's itself. It hath no other wings
  To spread abroad, nor eyes to see,
    Nor hands distinct to feel,
      Nor knees to kneel:
But being simple like the Deity
    In its own centre is a sphere
    Not shut up here, but everywhere.

It acts not from a centre to
          Its object as remote,
But present is when it doth view,
Being with the being it doth note.
          Whatever it doth do
It doth not by another engine work
But by itself which in the act doth lurk.
Its essence is transformed into a true
          And perfect act.
          And so exact
Hath God appeared in this mysterious fact
     That 'tis all eye, all act, all sight,
          And what it please can be,
               Not only see
Or do; for 'tis more voluble than light,
     Which can put on ten thousand forms,
     Being clothed with what itself adorns.

This made me present evermore
          With whatsoe'er I saw.
An object if it were before
My eye was by Dame Nature's law
          Within my soul. Her store
Was all at once within me; all her treasures
Were my immediate and internal pleasures,
Substantial joys which did inform my mind.
          With all she wrought
          My soul was fraught,
And every object in my soul a thought
     Begot, or was; I could not tell
          Whether the things did there
               Themselves appear
Which in my spirit truly seemed to dwell,
     Or whether my conforming mind
     Were not even all that therein shined.

But yet of this I was most sure,
  That at the utmost length
  (So worthy was it to endure)
  My soul could best express its strength;
   It was so quick and pure
That all my mind was wholly everywhere,
Whate'er it saw, 'twas ever wholly there;
The sun ten thousand legions off was nigh;
   The utmost star
   Though seen from far
Was present in the apple of my eye.
  There was my sight, my life, my sense,
   My substance and my mind.
    My spirit shined
Even there, not by a transient influence.
  The act was immanent, yet there;
  The thing remote, yet felt even here.

  O joy! O wonder and delight!
   O sacred mystery!
  My soul a spirit infinite!
  An image of the Deity!
   A pure, substantial light!
That being greatest which doth nothing seem!
Why, 'twas my all, I nothing did esteem
But that alone. A strange, mysterious sphere!
   A deep abyss
   That sees and is
The only proper place or bower of bliss.
  To its Creator 'tis so near
   In love and excellence,
   In life and sense,
In greatness, worth and nature; and so dear:
  In it, without hyperbole,
  The son and friend of God we see.

A strange, extended orb of joy,
　　Proceeding from within,
Which did on every side convey
Itself, and being nigh of kin
　　To God did every way
Dilate itself even in an instant, and
Like an indivisible centre stand
At once surrounding all eternity.
　　　　'Twas not a sphere
　　　　Yet did appear
One infinite. 'Twas somewhat everywhere.
　　And though it had a power to see
　　　　Far more, yet still it shined
　　　　And was a mind
Exerted, for it saw infinity:
　　'Twas not a sphere, but 'twas a power
　　Invisible, and yet a bower.

　　O wondrous self! O sphere of light,
　　　　O sphere of joy most fair;
　　O act, O power infinite,
　　O subtle and unbounded air!
　　　　O living orb of sight!
Thou which within me art, yet me! Thou eye
And temple of His whole infinity!
O what a world art thou! a world within!
　　　　All things appear,
　　　　All objects are
Alive in thee! Supersubstantial, rare,
　　Above themselves, and nigh of kin
　　　　To those pure things we find
　　　　In His great mind
Who made the world, though now eclipsed by sin.
　　There they are useful and divine,
　　Exalted there they ought to shine.

NATURE

That custom is a second nature, we
Most plainly find by nature's purity.
For nature teacheth nothing but the truth;
I'm sure mine did in my virgin youth.
The very day my spirit did inspire,
The world's fair beauty set my soul on fire.
My senses were informers to my heart,
The conduits of His glory, power and art.
His greatness, wisdom, goodness I did see,
His glorious love, and His eternity,
Almost as soon as born; and every sense
Was in me like to some intelligence.
I was by nature prone and apt to love
All light and beauty, both in heaven above
And earth beneath, prone even to admire,
Adore and praise as well as to desire.
My inclinations raised me up on high
And guided me to all infinity.
A secret self I had enclosed within
That was not bounded with my clothes or skin
Or terminated with my sight, the sphere
Of which was bounded with the heavens here:
But that did rather, like the subtle light,
Secured from rough and raging storms by night,
Break through the lantern's sides, and freely ray
Dispersing and dilating every way;
Whose steady beams, too subtle for the wind,
Are such that we their bounds can scarcely find.
It did encompass and possess rare things,
But yet felt more, and on its angels' wings
Pierced through the skies immediately and sought
For all that could beyond all worlds be thought.
It did not move nor one way go but stood,
And by dilating of itself all good
It strove to see, as if 'twere present there,

Even while it present stood conversing here,
And more suggested than I could discern
Or ever since by any means could learn.
Vast, uneffected, wonderful desires,
Like inward, native, uncaused, hidden fires,
Sprang up with expectations very strange,
Which into new desires did quickly change.
For all I saw beyond the azure round
Was endless darkness with no beauty crowned.
Why beauty should not there as well as here,
Why goodness should not likewise there appear,
Why treasures and delights should bounded be
Since there is such a wide infinity—
These were the doubts and troubles of my soul,
By which I do perceive without control
A world of endless joys by nature made,
That needs must flourish ever, never fade.
A wide, magnificent and spacious sky,
So rich, 'tis worthy of the Deity,
Clouds here and there like wingèd chariots flying,
Flowers ever flourishing yet always dying,
A day of glory where I all things see,
As 'twere enriched with beams of light for me,
And drowned in glorious rays of purer light
Succeeded with a black yet glorious night,
Stars sweetly shedding to my pleasèd sense
On all things their nocturnal influence,
With secret rooms in times and ages more
Past and to come enlarging my great store—
These all, in order present unto me,
My happy eyes did in a moment see
With wonders thereto, to my soul unknown,
Till they by men and reading first were shown.
All which were made that I might ever be
With some great workman, some great Deity.
But yet there were new rooms and spaces more
Beyond all these, wide regions o'er and o'er,

And into them my pent-up soul like fire
Did break, surmounting all I here admire.
The spaces filled were, like a cabinet
Of joys before me most distinctly set;
The empty, like to large and vacant room
For fancy to enlarge in and presume
A space for more, removed, but yet adorning
These near at hand, that pleased me every morning.
Here I was seated to behold new things
In the fair fabric of the King of kings.
All, all was mine. The fountain though not known,
Yet that there must be one was plainly shown.
Which fountain of delights must needs be love
As all the goodness of the things did prove.
It shines upon me from the highest skies,
And all its creatures for my sake doth prize,
Of whose enjoyment I am made the end;
While how the same is so I comprehend.

THE PERSON

        Ye sacred limbs
    A richer blazon I will lay
        On you than first I found:
        That like celestial kings
    Ye might with ornaments of joy
        Be always crowned.
    A deep vermilion on a red,
    On that a scarlet I will lay,
        With gold I'll crown your head
        Which like the sun shall ray.
    With robes of glory and delight
        I'll make you bright.
Mistake me not, I do not mean to bring
    New robes, but to display the thing;
Nor paint, nor clothe, nor crown, nor add a ray,
But glorify by taking all away.

The naked things
Are most sublime and brightest show
    When they alone are seen:
    Men's hands than angels' wings
Are truer wealth even here below;
    For those but seem.
Their worth they then do best reveal
When we all metaphors remove,
    For metaphors conceal
    And only vapours prove.
They best are blazoned when we see
    The anatomy;
Survey the skin, cut up the flesh, the veins
    Unfold: the glory there remains.
The muscles, fibres, arteries and bones
Are better far than crowns and precious stones.

    Shall I not then
Delight in these most sacred treasures
    Which my great father gave
    Far more than other men
Delight in gold? Since these are pleasures
    That make us brave!
Far braver than the pearl or gold
That glitter on a lady's neck!
    The rubies we behold,
    The diamonds that deck
The hands of queens compared unto
    The hands we view;
The softer lilies and the roses are
    Less ornaments to those that wear
The same than are the hands and lips and eyes
Of those who those false ornaments so prize.

    Let verity
Be thy delight; let me esteem
    True wealth far more than toys;

Let sacred riches be,
While falser treasures only seem,
My real joys.
For golden chains and bracelets are
But gilded manacles whereby
Old Satan doth ensnare,
Allure, bewitch the eye.
Thy gifts, O God, alone I'll prize,
My tongue, my eyes,
My cheeks, my lips, my ears, my hands, my feet,
Their harmony is far more sweet;
Their beauty true. And these in all my ways
Shall themes become, and organs of thy praise.

LOVE

O nectar! O delicious stream!
O ravishing and only pleasure! Where
Shall such another theme
Inspire my tongue with joys or please mine ear?
Abridgement of delights,
And queen of sights!
O mine of rarities! O kingdom wide!
O more! O cause of all! O glorious bride!
O God! O bride of God! O King!
O soul and crown of everything!

Did not I covet to behold
Some endless monarch that did always live
In palaces of gold,
Willing all kingdoms, realms and crowns to give
Unto my soul? Whose love
A spring might prove
Of endless glories, honours, friendships, pleasures,
Joys, praises, beauties and celestial treasures?
Lo, now I see there's such a king,
The fountain head of everything!

Did my ambition ever dream
Of such a lord, of such a love? Did I
    Expect so sweet a stream
As this at any time? Could any eye
      Believe it? Why, all power
        Is usèd here
Joys down from heaven on my head to shower
And Jove beyond the fiction doth appear
    Once more in golden rain to come
    To Danae's pleasing, fruitful womb.

    His Ganymede! His life! His joy!
Or He comes down to me or takes me up
    That I might be His boy,
And fill, and taste, and give, and drink the cup.
    But these (though great) are all
      Too short and small,
Too weak and feeble to express
The true, mysterious depths of blessedness.
    I am His image and His friend;
    His son, bride, glory, temple, end.

THE RAPTURE

    Sweet Infancy!
O fire of heaven! O sacred light!
    How fair and bright!
    How great am I,
Whom all the world doth magnify!

    O heavenly joy!
O great and sacred blessèdness
    Which I possess!
    So great a joy
Who did into my arms convey?

From God above
Being sent, the heavens me enflame
To praise His name.
The stars do move!
The burning sun doth show His love.

O how divine
Am I! To all this sacred wealth,
This life and health,
Who raised? Who mine
Did make the same? What hand divine!

DESIRE

For giving me desire,
An eager thirst, a burning, ardent fire,
A virgin, infant flame,
A love with which into the world I came,
An inward, hidden, heavenly love
Which in my soul did work and move
And ever, ever me inflame
With restless longing, heavenly avarice
That never could be satisfied,
That did incessantly a paradise
Unknown suggest, and some thing undescried
Discern, and bear me to it; be
Thy name forever praised by me.

My parched and withered bones
Burnt up did seem; my soul was full of groans;
My thoughts extensions were,
Like paces, reaches, steps they did appear,
They somewhat hotly did pursue,
Knew that they had not all their due,
Nor ever quiet were
But made my flesh like hungry, thirsty ground,

My heart a deep, profound abyss,
And every joy and pleasure but a wound
So long as I my blessèdness did miss.
O happiness! A famine burns,
And all my life to anguish turns!

Where are the silent streams,
The living waters and the glorious beams,
The sweet, reviving bowers,
The shady groves, the sweet and curious flowers,
The springs and trees, the heavenly days,
The flowery meads, the glorious rays,
The gold and silver towers?
Alas, all these are poor and empty things,
Trees, waters, days and shining beams,
Fruits, flowers, bowers, shady groves and springs
No joy will yield, no more than silent streams.
These are but dead, material toys,
And cannot make my heavenly joys.

O love! Ye amities
And friendships that appear above the skies!
Ye feasts and living pleasures!
Ye senses, honours and imperial treasures!
Ye bridal joys! ye high delights
That satisfy all appetites!
Ye sweet affections and
Ye high respects! Whatever joys there be
In triumphs, whatsoever stand
In amicable, sweet society,
Whatever pleasures are at His right hand
Ye must, before I am divine,
In full propriety be mine.

This soaring, sacred thirst,
Ambassador of bliss, approachèd first,
Making a place in me

That made me apt to prize and taste and see,
　　For not the objects but the sense
　　　Of things doth bliss to souls dispense
　　　　And make it lord like thee.
　Sense, feeling, taste, complacency and sight,
　　These are the true and real joys,
　The living, flowing, inward, melting, bright
　And heavenly pleasures; all the rest are toys;
　　All which are founded in desire,
　　As light in flame and heat in fire.

ON NEWS

　News from a foreign country came
As if my treasure and my wealth lay there:
　So much it did my heart enflame!
'Twas wont to call my soul into mine ear
　　　Which thither went to meet
　　　　The approaching sweet,
　　　And on the threshold stood
　To entertain the unknown good.
　　　　It hovered there
　　　As if 'twould leave mine ear,
And was so eager to embrace
The joyful tidings as they came,
'Twould almost leave its dwelling place
　　　To entertain the same.

　　As if the tidings were the things,
My very joys themselves, my foreign treasure,
　Or else did bear them on their wings;
With so much joy they came, with so much pleasure.
　　　My soul stood at the gate
　　　　To recreate
　　　Itself with bliss, and to
　Be pleased with speed. A fuller view

45

It fain would take
Yet journeys back would make
Unto my heart; as if 'twould fain
Go out to meet, yet stay within
To fit a place, to entertain,
    And bring the tidings in.

What sacred instinct did inspire
My soul in childhood with a hope so strong?
What secret force moved my desire
To expect my joys beyond the seas, so young?
    Felicity I knew
    Was out of view:
    And being here alone
I saw that happiness was gone
    From me! for this,
I thirsted absent bliss
And thought that sure beyond the seas,
Or else in something near at hand
I knew not yet, (since naught did please
    I knew) my bliss did stand.

But little did the infant dream
That all the treasures of the world were by,
And that himself was so the cream
And crown of all which round about did lie.
    Yet thus it was. The gem,
    The diadem,
    The ring enclosing all
That stood upon this earhty ball,
    The heavenly eye
    Much wider than the sky
Wherein they all included were,
The glorious soul that was the king
Made to possess them, did appear
    A small and little thing!

THE RETURN

To infancy, O Lord, again I come,
    That I my manhood may improve:
My early tutor is the womb,
    I still my cradle love.
'Tis strange that I should wisest be
When least I could an error see.

Till I gain strength against temptation I
    Perceive it safest to abide
An infant still, and therefore fly
    (A lowly state may hide
A man from danger) to the womb,
That I may yet new-born become.

My God, thy bounty then did ravish me!
    Before I learnèd to be poor,
I always did thy riches see
    And thankfully adore:
Thy glory and thy goodness were
My sweet companions all the year.

THE APOSTASY

One star
Is better far
Than many precious stones:
One sun, which is above in glory seen,
    Is worth ten thousand golden thrones:
A juicy herb or spire of grass
In useful virtue, native green,
    An emerald doth surpass,
Hath in't more value, though less seen.

No wars,
Nor mortal jars,
Nor bloody feuds, nor coin,
Nor griefs which they occasion saw I then;
Nor wicked thieves which this purloin;
I had no thoughts that were impure,
Esteeming both women and men
God's work, I was secure,
And reckoned peace my choicest gem.

As Eve
I did believe
Myself in Eden set,
Affecting neither gold nor ermined crowns,
Nor aught else that I need forget;
No mud did foul my limpid streams,
No mist eclipsed my sun with frowns;
Set off with heavenly beams
My joys were meadows, fields and towns.

Those things
Which cherubins
Did not at first behold
Among God's works, which Adam did not see,
As robes, and stones enchased in gold,
Rich cabinets, and such like fine
Inventions, could not ravish me;
I thought not bowls of wine
Needful for my felicity.

All bliss
Consists in this,
To do as Adam did;
And not to know those superficial joys
Which were from him in Eden hid;
Those little, new-invented things,
Fine lace and silks, such childish toys

As ribbons are and rings,
Or worldly pelf that us destroys.

For God,
Both great and good,
The seeds of melancholy
Created not; but only foolish men
Grown mad with customary folly
Which doth increase their wants, so dote
As when they elder grow they then
Such baubles chiefly note,
More fools at twenty years than ten.

But I,
I knew not why,
Did learn among them too
At length; and when I once with blemished eyes
Began their pence and toys to view,
Drowned in their customs, I became
A stranger to the shining skies,
Lost as a dying flame,
And hobby-horses brought to prize.

The sun
And moon forgone,
As if unmade, appear
No more to me; to God and heaven dead
I was, as though they never were;
Upon some useless, gaudy book,
When what I knew of God was fled,
The child being taught to look,
His soul was quickly murderèd.

O fine!
O most divine!
O brave! they cried, and showed
Some tinsel thing whose glittering did amaze,

And to their cries its beauty owed;
Thus I on riches, by degrees,
Of a new stamp did learn to gaze;
    While all the world for these
I lost, my joy turned to a blaze.

SOLITUDE

    How desolate!
Ah! how forlorn, how sadly did I stand
    When in the field my woeful state
        I felt! Not all the land,
            Not all the skies,
    Though heaven shined before mine eyes,
Could comfort yield in any field to me,
Nor could my mind contentment find or see.

    Removed from town,
From people, churches, feasts and holidays,
    The sword of state, the mayor's gown,
        And all the neighbouring boys;
            As if no kings
    On earth there were, or living things,
The silent skies salute mine eyes, the seas
My soul surround; no rest I found, or ease.

    My roving mind
Searched every corner of the spacious earth,
    From sky to sky, if it could find
        (But found not) any mirth:
            Not all the coasts,
    Nor all the great and glorious hosts
In heaven or earth did comfort me afford;
I pined for hunger at a plenteous board.

I do believe,
The evening being shady and obscure,
The very silence did me grieve
And sorrow more procure:
A secret want
Did make me think my fortune scant.
I was so blind, I could not find my health,
No joy mine eye could there espy, nor wealth.

Nor could I guess
What kind of thing I longed for; but that I
Did somewhat lack of blessèdness,
Beside the earth and sky,
I plainly found;
It grieved me much, I felt a wound
Perplex me sore; yet what my store should be
I did not know, nothing would show to me.

Ye sullen things!
Ye dumb, ye silent creatures and unkind!
How can I call you pleasant springs
Unless ye ease my mind!
Will ye not speak
What 'tis I want, nor silence break?
O pity me and let me see some joy;
Some kindness show to me, although a boy.

They silent stood;
Nor earth, nor woods, nor hills, nor brooks, nor skies,
Would tell me where the hidden good
Which I did long for lies:
The shady trees,
The evening dark, the humming bees,
The chirping birds, mute springs and fords, conspire
To give no answer unto my desire.

Bells ringing I
Far off did hear, some country church they spake;

The noise re-echoing through the sky
   My melancholy brake;
     When't reached mine ear
   Some tidings thence I hoped to hear:
But not a bell me news could tell, or show
My longing mind, where joys to find, or know.

     I grieved the more
'Cause I thereby somewhat encouraged was
   That I from those should learn my store;
     For churches are a place
     That nearer stand
   Than any part of all the land
To heaven; from whence some little sense I might
To help my mind receive and find some light.

     They louder sound
Than men do talk, something they should disclose;
   The empty sound did therefore wound
     Because not show repose.
     It did revive
   To think that men were there alive;
But had my soul, called by the toll, gone in
I might have found, to ease my wound, a thing.

     A little ease
Perhaps, but that might more molest my mind;
   One flattering drop would more disease
     My soul with thirst, and grind
     My heart with grief:
   For people can yield no relief
In public sort when in that court they shine,
Except they move my soul with love divine.

     Th'external rite,
Although the face be wondrous sweet and fair,
   Will never sate my appetite

No more than empty air
    Yield solid food.
  Must I the best and highest good
Seek to possess, or blessèdness in vain
(Though 'tis alive in some place) strive to gain?

        O what would I
Diseasèd, wanting, melancholy, give
    To find what is felicity,
        The place where bliss doth live?
            Those regions fair
    Which are not lodged in sea nor air,
Nor woods, nor fields, nor arbour yields, nor springs,
Nor heavens show to us below, nor kings.

        I might have gone
Into the city, market, tavern, street,
    Yet only change my station,
        And strove in vain to meet
            That ease of mind
    Which all alone I longed to find:
A common inn doth no such thing betray,
Nor doth it walk in people's talk or play.

        O Eden fair!
Where shall I seek the soul of holy joy
    Since I to find it here despair;
        Nor in the shining day,
            Nor in the shade,
    Nor in the field, nor in a trade
I can it see. Felicity! O where
Shall I thee find to ease my mind! O where!

BELLS

Hark! hark, my soul! the bells do ring,
    And with a louder voice
Call many families to sing
His public praises and rejoice:
Their shriller sound doth wound the air,
Their grosser strokes affect the ear
That we might thither all repair
    And more divine ones hear.
        If lifeless earth
        Can make such mirth,
What then shall souls above the starry sphere!

Bells are but clay that men refine
    And raise from duller ore;
Yet now, as if they were divine,
They call whole cities to adore;
Exalted into steeples they
Disperse their sound, and from on high
Chime in our souls; they every way
    Speak to us through the sky;
        Their iron tongues
        Do utter songs,
And shall our stony hearts make no reply!

From darker mines and earthy caves
    At last let souls awake,
And rousing from obscurer graves
From lifeless bells example take;
Lifted above all earthly cares,
Let them (like these) raised up on high,
Forsaking all the baser wares
    Of dull mortality
        His praises sing,
        Tunably ring,
In a less distance from the peaceful sky.

CHRISTENDOM

When first mine infant ear
Of Christendom did hear
I much admired what kind of place or thing
It was of which the folk did talk:
What coast, what region, what therein
Did move, or might be seen to walk.
My great desire
Like ardent fire
Did long to know what things did lie behind
The mystic name, to which mine eye was blind.

Some depth it did conceal,
Which, till it did reveal
Itself to me, no quiet, peace or rest
Could I by any means attain;
My earnest thoughts did me molest
Till someone should the thing explain:
I thought it was
A glorious place
Where souls might dwell in all delight and bliss;
So thought, yet feared lest I the truth might miss.

Among ten thousand things,
Gold, silver, cherubs' wings,
Pearls, rubies, diamonds, a church with spires,
Masks, stages, games and plays,
That then might suit my young desires,
Fine feathers, farthings, holidays,
Cards, music, dice,
So much in price;
A city did before mine eyes present
Itself, wherein there reignèd sweet content.

A town beyond the seas
Whose prospect much did please,

And to my soul so sweetly raise delight
   As if a long expected joy,
   Shut up in that transforming sight,
   Would into me itself convey;
       And blessèdness
       I there possess,
As if that city stood on real ground,
And all the profit mine which there was found.

    Whatever force me led,
    My spirit sweetly fed
On these conceits; that 'twas a city strange,
   Wherein I saw no gallant inns,
   No markets, shops or old exchange,
   No childish trifles, useless things;
       No wall nor bounds
       That town surrounds,
But as if all its streets even endless were
Without or gate or wall it did appear.

    Things native sweetly grew
    Which there mine eye did view,
Plain, simple, cheap, on either side the street,
   Which was exceeding fair and wide;
   Sweet mansions there mine eyes did meet,
   Green trees the shaded doors did hide;
       My chiefest joys
       Were girls and boys
That in those streets still up and down did play,
Which crowned the town with constant holiday.

    A sprightly, pleasant time
    (Even summer in its prime),
Did gild the trees, the houses, children, skies,
   And made the city all divine;
   It ravishèd my wondering eyes
   To see the sun so brightly shine;

The heat and light
Seemed in my sight
With such a dazzling lustre shed on them,
As made me think 'twas th' New Jerusalem.

Beneath the lofty trees
I saw, of all degrees,
Folk calmly sitting in their doors, while some
Did standing with them kindly talk,
Some smile, some sing, or what was done
Observe, while others by did walk;
They viewed the boys
And girls, their joys,
The streets adorning with their angel-faces,
Themselves diverting in those pleasant places.

The streets like lanes did seem
Not paved with stones, but green,
Which with red clay did partly mixed appear;
'Twas holy ground of great esteem;
The springs choice liveries did wear
Of verdant grass that grew between
The purling streams,
Which golden beams
Of light did varnish, coming from the sun,
By which to distant realms was service done.

In fresh and cooler rooms
Retired they dine; perfumes
They wanted not, having the pleasant shade
And peace to bless their house within,
By sprinkled waters cooler made
For those incarnate cherubin.
This happy place
With all the grace,
The joy and beauty which it did beseem,
Did ravish me and heighten my esteem.

That here to raise desire
All objects do conspire,
People in years, and young enough to play,
　Their streets of houses, common peace,
　In one continued holiday
Whose gladsome mirth shall never cease:
　　Since these become
　　My Christendom,
What learn I more than that Jerusalem
Is mine, as 'tis my Maker's, choicest gem.

　　Before I was aware
　　Truth did to me appear,
And represented to my virgin eyes
　Th'unthought of joys and treasures
　Wherein my bliss and glory lies;
　My God's delight (which gives me measure)
　　His turtle dove
　　Is peace and love
In towns; for holy children, maids and men
Make up the king of glory's diadem.

SHADOWS IN THE WATER

In unexperienced infancy
Many a sweet mistake doth lie,
Mistake though false, intending true,
A seeming somewhat more than view
　That doth instruct the mind
　In things that lie behind,
And many secrets to us show
Which afterwards we come to know.

Thus did I by the water's brink
Another world beneath me think,
And while the lofty spacious skies

Reversèd there abused mine eyes,
    I fancied other feet
    Came mine to touch and meet;
As by some puddle I did play
Another world within it lay.

Beneath the water people drowned,
Yet with another heaven crowned,
In spacious regions seemed to go
Freely moving to and fro;
    In bright and open space
    I saw their very face;
Eyes, hands and feet they had like mine;
Another sun did with them shine.

'Twas strange that people there should walk
And yet I could not hear them talk;
That through a little watery chink
Which one dry ox or horse might drink
    We other worlds should see,
    Yet not admitted be;
And other confines there behold
Of light and darkness, heat and cold.

I called them oft, but called in vain,
No speeches we could entertain;
Yet did I there expect to find
Some other world to please my mind.
    I plainly saw by these
    A new antipodes,
Whom, though they were so plainly seen,
A film kept off that stood between.

By walking men's reversèd feet
I chanced another world to meet;
Though it did not to view exceed
A phantasm, 'tis a world indeed

Where skies beneath us shine
And earth by art divine
Another face presents below,
Where people's feet against ours go.

Within the regions of the air,
Compassed about with heavens fair,
Great tracts of land there may be found
Enriched with fields and fertile ground;
Where many numerous hosts
In those far distant coasts,
For other great and glorious ends,
Inhabit, my yet unkown friends.

O ye that stand upon the brink,
Whom I so near me, through the chink,
With wonder see; what faces there,
Whose feet, whose bodies, do ye wear?
I my companions see
In you, another me.
They seemèd others, but are we;
Our second selves those shadows be.

Look how far off those lower skies
Extend themselves! Scarce with mine eyes
I can them reach. O ye my friends
What secret borders on those ends?
Are lofty heavens hurled
'Bout your inferior world?
Are ye the representatives
Of other people's distant lives?

Of all the playmates which I knew
That here I do the image view
In other selves; what can it mean?
But that below the purling stream
Some unknown joys there be

Laid up in store for me;
To which I shall, when that thin skin
Is broken, be admitted in.

ON LEAPING OVER THE MOON

I saw new worlds beneath the water lie,
   New people, and another sky
      And sun, which seen by day
      Might things more clear display.
        Just such another
        Of late my brother
Did in his travel see, and saw by night
   A much more strange and wondrous sight;
Nor could the world exhibit such another,
   So great a sight, but in a brother.

Adventure strange! No such in story we
   New or old, true or feignèd see.
      On earth he seemed to move
      Yet heaven went above;
        Up in the skies
        His body flies
In open, visible, yet magic, sort;
   As he along the way did sport
Like Icarus over the flood he soars
   Without the help of wings or oars.

As he went tripping o'er the king's highway
   A little pearly river lay
      O'er which, without a wing
      Or oar, he dared to swim,
        Swim through the air
        On body fair;

He would not use nor trust Icarian wings
   Lest they should prove deceitful things;
For had he fall'n it had been wondrous high,
   Not from, but from above, the sky.

He might have dropped through that thin element
   Into a fathomless descent
     Unto the nether sky
     That did beneath him lie,
       And there might tell
       What wonders dwell
On earth above. Yet bold he briskly runs
   And soon the danger overcomes;
Who, as he leapt, with joy related soon
   How *happy he* o'er-leapt the moon.

What wondrous things upon the earth are done
   Beneath, and yet above, the sun?
     Deeds all appear again
     In higher spheres; remain
       In clouds as yet;
       But there they get
Another light, and in another way
   Themselves to us above display.
The skies themselves this earthly globe surround,
   We are even here within them found.

On heavenly ground within the skies we walk
   And in this middle centre talk;
     Did we but wisely move,
     On earth in heaven above,
       We then should be
       Exalted high
Above the sky; from whence whoever falls
   Through a long, dismal precipice,
Sinks to the deep abyss where Satan crawls
   Where horrid death and despair lies.

As much as others thought themselves to lie
        Beneath the moon, so much more high
            Himself he thought to fly
            Above the starry sky,
                As that he spied
                Below the tide.
Thus did he yield me in the shady night
        A wondrous and instructive light,
Which taught me that under our feet there is,
        As o'er our heads, a place of bliss.

     *   *   *

To the same purpose; he, not long before
        Brought home from nurse, going to the door
            To do some little thing
            He must not do within,
                With wonder cries,
                As in the skies
He saw the moon, 'O yonder is the moon
        Newly come after me to town,
That shined at Lugwardin but yesternight,
        Where I enjoyed the self-same light.'

As if it had even twenty thousand faces
        It shines at once in many places;
            To all the earth so wide
            God doth the stars divide,
                With so much art
                The moon impart,
They serve us all, serve wholly everyone
        As if they servèd him alone.
While every single person hath such store
        'Tis want of sense that makes us poor.

DREAMS

'Tis strange! I saw the skies,
I saw the hills before mine eyes,
The sparrow fly,
The lands that did about me lie,
The real sun, that heavenly eye!
Can closed eyes even in the darkest night
See through their lids and be informed with sight?

The people were to me
As true as those by day I see;
As true the air,
The earth as sweet, as fresh, as fair
As that which did by day repair
Unto my waking sense! Can all the sky,
Can all the world, within my brain-pan lie?

What sacred secret's this
Which seems to intimate my bliss?
What is there in
The narrow confines of my skin
That is alive and feels within
When I am dead? Can magnitude possess
An active memory, yet not be less?

May all that I can see
Awake, by night within me be?
My childhood knew
No difference, but all was true,
As real all as what I view;
The world itself was there. 'Twas wondrous strange
That heaven and earth should so their place exchange.

Till that which vulgar sense
Doth falsely call experience
Distinguished things,

The ribbons and the gaudy wings
    Of birds, the virtues and the sins
That represented were in dreams by night
As really my senses did delight,

    Or grieve, as those I saw
    By day; things terrible did awe
        My soul with fear;
    The apparitions seemed as near
    As things could be, and things they were:
Yet were they all by fancy in me wrought,
And all their being founded in a thought.

    O what a thing is thought!
    Which seems a dream; yea, seemeth naught,
        Yet doth the mind
    Affect as much as what we find
    Most near and true! Sure men are blind
And can't the forcible reality
Of things that secret are within them see.

    Thoughts! Surely thoughts are true,
    They please as much as things can do:
        Nay things are dead,
    And in themselves are severèd
    From souls, nor can they fill the head
Without our thoughts. Thoughts are the real things
From whence all joy, from whence all sorrow springs.

INSATIABLENESS

1

No walls confine! Can nothing hold my mind?
Can I no rest nor satisfaction find?
    Must I behold eternity
        And see

What things above the heavens be?
　　Will nothing serve the turn?
　　Nor earth, nor seas, nor skies?
　　　　Till I what lies
　　　In time's beginning find,
　　Must I till then forever burn?

Not all the crowns, not all the heaps of gold
On earth, not all the tales that can be told
　　Will satisfaction yield to me:
　　　　Nor tree,
　　Nor shade, nor sun, nor Eden, be
　　　A joy; nor gems in gold,
　　　(Be't pearl or precious stone),
　　　　Nor spring, nor flowers,
　　　Answer my craving powers,
　　Nor anything that eyes behold.

Till I what was before all time descry,
The world's beginning seems but vanity.
　　My soul doth there long thoughts extend;
　　　　No end
　　Doth find, or being comprehend;
　　　Yet somewhat sees that is
　　　The obscure, shady face
　　　　Of endless space,
　　　All room within, where I
　　Expect to meet eternal bliss.

2
This busy, vast, enquiring soul
　　Brooks no control,
　　No limits will endure
　　Nor any rest: it will all see,
Not time alone, but even eternity.
　　What is it? Endless, sure.

'Tis mean ambition to desire
    A single world;
To many I aspire,
    Though one upon another hurled;
Nor will they all, if they be all confined,
    Delight my mind.

This busy, vast, enquiring soul
    Brooks no control,
    'Tis hugely curious too.
Each one of all those worlds must be
Enriched with infinite variety
    And worth, or 'twill not do.

'Tis nor delight nor perfect pleasure
    To have a purse
That hath a bottom of its treasure,
Since I must thence endless expense disburse.
Sure there's a God (for else there's no delight)
    One infinite.

HOSANNA

No more shall walls, no more shall walls confine
That glorious soul which in my flesh doth shine:
    No more shall walls of clay or mud
        Nor ceilings made of wood,
    Nor crystal windows bound my sight,
    But rather shall admit delight.
        The skies that seem to bound
        My joys and treasures,
    Of more endearing pleasures
        Themselves become a ground:
While from the centre to the utmost sphere
My goods are multiplièd everywhere.

The Deity, the Deity to me
Doth all things give, and make me clearly see
   The moon and stars, the air and sun
      Into my chamber come;
   The seas and rivers hither flow,
    Yea, here the trees of Eden grow,
      The fowls and fishes stand,
        Kings and their thrones,
     As 'twere at my command;
     God's wealth, His holy ones,
The ages too, and angels, all conspire:
While I, that I the centre am, admire.

No more, no more shall clouds eclipse my treasures,
Nor viler shades obscure my highest pleasures;
   No more shall earthen husks confine
    My blessings which do shine
  Within the skies, or else above:
  Both worlds, one heaven made by love,
     In common happy I
       With angels walk
    And there my joys espy;
    With God himself I talk,
Wondering with ravishment all things to see
Such real joys, so truly mine, to be.

No more shall trunks and dishes be my store,
Nor ropes of pearl, nor chains of golden ore;
   As if such beings yet were not,
    They all shall be forgot.
  No such in Eden did appear,
  No such in heaven; heaven here
    Would be, were those removed;
      The sons of men
    Live in Jerusalem,
    Had they not baubles loved.

These clouds dispersed, the heavens clear I see.
Wealth new-invented mine shall never be.

Transcendent objects doth my God provide,
In such convenient order all contrived,
    That all things in their proper place
      My soul doth best embrace,
    Extends its arms beyond the seas,
    Above the heavens itself can please,
      With God enthroned may reign;
        Like sprightly streams
      My thoughts on things remain,
      Or else like vital beams
They reach to, shine on, quicken things, and make
Them truly useful; while I all partake.

For me the world created was by love;
For me the skies, the seas, the sun do move;
    The earth for me doth stable stand;
      For me each fruitful land
    For me the very angels God made His
    And my companions in bliss:
      His laws command all men
        That they love me,
      Under a penalty
      Severe, in case they miss:
His laws require His creatures all to praise
His name, and when they do't be most my joys.

AN HYMN UPON ST. BARTHOLOMEW'S DAY

      What powerful spirit lives within!
    What active angel doth inhabit here!
      What heavenly light inspires my skin
    Which doth so like a Deity appear!
    A living temple of all ages I

Within me see
A temple of eternity!
All kingdoms I descry
In me.

An inward omnipresence here,
Mysteriously like His, within me stands;
Whose knowledge is a sacred sphere,
That in itself at once includes all lands.
There is some angel that within me can
Both talk and move
And walk and fly and see and love
A man on earth, a man
Above.

Dull walls of clay my spirit leaves
And in a foreign kingdom doth appear,
This great apostle it receives,
Admires his works and sees them, standing here.
Within myself from east to west I move
As if I were
At once a cherubim and sphere,
Or was at once above,
And here.

The soul's a messenger whereby
Within our inward temple we may be
Even like the very Deity,
In all the parts of His eternity.
O live within and leave unwieldy dross!
Flesh is but clay!
O fly my soul and haste away
To Jesus' throne or cross.
Obey!

When thou dost take
    this sacred book into thy hand;
Think not that thou
    th'included sense dost understand.

It is a sign
    thou wantest sound intelligence
If that thou think
    thyself to understand the sense.

Be not deceived
    thou then on it in vain may'st gaze
The way is intricate
    that leads into a maze.

Here's naught but what's mysterious
    to an understanding eye;
Where reverence alone stands ope,
    and sense stands by.

1

An empty book is like an infant's soul, in which anything may be written. It is capable of all things but containeth nothing. I have a mind to fill this with profitable wonders. And since love made you put it into my hands I will fill it with those truths you love, without knowing them; and with those things which, if it be possible, shall show my love; to you, in communicating most enriching truths; to truth, in exalting her beauties in such a soul.

2

Do not wonder that I promise to fill it with those truths you love but know not; for though it be a maxim in the schools that there is no love of a thing unknown, yet I have found that things unknown have a secret influence on the soul, and like the centre of the earth unseen, violently attract it. We love we know not what, and therefore everything allures us. As iron at a distance is drawn by the loadstone, there being some invisible communications between them, so is there in us a world of love to somewhat, though we know not what in the world that should be. There are invisible ways of conveyance, by which some great thing doth touch our souls, and by which we tend to it. Do you not feel yourself drawn with the expectation and desire of some great thing?

3

I will open my mouth in parables: I will utter things that have been kept secret from the foundation of the world. Things strange, yet common; incredible, yet known; most high, yet plain; infinitely profitable, but not esteemed. Is it not a great thing that you should be heir of the world? Is it not a very enriching verity? In which the fellowship of the mystery, which from the beginning of the world hath been hid in God, lies concealed! The thing hath been from the creation of the world, but hath not been so explained as that the interior beauty should be understood. It is my design therefore in such a plain manner to unfold it that my friendship may appear in making you possessor of the whole world.

4

I will not by the noise of bloody wars and the dethroning of kings advance you to glory, but by the gentle ways of peace and love. As a deep friendship meditates and intends the deepest designs for the advancement of its objects, so doth it show itself in choosing the sweetest and most delightful methods, whereby not to weary but please the person it desireth to advance. Where love administers physic its tenderness is expressed in balms and cordials. It hateth corrosives and is rich in its administrations. Even so God, designing to show His love in exalting you, hath chosen the ways of ease and repose, by which you should ascend. And I after His similitude will lead you into paths plain and familiar; where all envy, rapine, bloodshed, complaint and malice shall be far removed, and nothing appear but contentment and thanksgiving. Yet shall the end be so glorious that angels durst not hope for so great a one till they had seen it.

16

That all the world is yours, your very senses and the inclinations of your mind declare. The works of God manifest, His laws testify and His word doth prove it. His attributes most sweetly make it evident. The powers of your soul confirm it. So that in the midst of such rich demonstrations you may infinitely delight in God as your father, friend and benefactor, in yourself as His heir, child and bride, in the whole world as the gift and token of His love. Neither can anything but ignorance destroy your joys, for if you know yourself, or God, or the world, you must of necessity enjoy it.

19

You never know yourself till you know more than your body. The image of God was not seated in the features of your face, but in the lineaments of your soul. In the knowledge of your powers, inclinations and principles, the knowledge of yourself chiefly consisteth. Which are so great that even to the most learned of men their greatness is incredible, and so divine that they are infinite in value. Alas, the world is but a little centre in comparison of you. Suppose it millions of miles from the earth to the heavens, and millions of millions above the stars, both here and over the heads of our antipodes: it is surrounded with infinite and eternal space. And like a gentleman's house to one that is travelling, it is a long time before you come unto it, you pass it in an instant, and leave it forever. The omnipresence and eternity of God are your fellows and companions, and all that is in them ought to be made your familiar treasures. Your understanding comprehends the world like the dust of a balance, measures heaven with a span and esteems a thousand years but as one day. So that great, endless, eternal delights are only fit to be its enjoyments.

25

Your enjoyment of the world is never right till you so esteem it that everything in it is more your treasure than a king's exchequer full of gold and silver. And that exchequer yours also in its place and service. Can you take too much joy in your Father's works? He is Himself in everything. Some things are little on the outside, and rough and common, but I remember the time when the dust of the streets were as precious as gold to my infant eyes, and now they are more precious to the eye of reason.

26

The services of things and their excellencies are spiritual, being objects not of the eye but of the mind; and you more spiritual by how much more you esteem them. Pigs eat acorns, but neither consider the sun that gave them life nor the influences of the heavens by which they were nourished, nor the very root of the tree from whence they came. This being the work of angels, who in a wide and clear light see even the sea that gave them moisture, and feed upon that acorn spiritually, while they know the ends for which it was created, and feast upon all these as upon a world of joys within it: while to ignorant swine that eat the shell it is an empty husk of no taste nor delightful savour.

27

You never enjoy the world aright till you see how a sand exhibiteth the wisdom and power of God, and prize in everything the service which they do you by manifesting His glory and goodness to your soul, far more than the visible beauty on their surface or the material

74

services they can do your body. Wine by its moisture quencheth my thirst whether I consider it or no, but to see it flowing from His love who gave it unto man quencheth the thirst even of the holy angels. To consider it is to drink it spiritually. To rejoice in its diffusion is to be of a public mind. And to take pleasure in all the benefits it doth to all is heavenly, for so they do in heaven. To do so is to be divine and good, and to imitate our infinite and eternal Father.

28

Your enjoyment of the world is never right till every morning you awake in heaven, see yourself in your Father's palace, and look upon the skies and the earth and the air as celestial joys, having such a reverend esteem of all as if you were among the angels. The bride of a monarch in her husband's chamber hath no such causes of delight as you.

29

You never enjoy the world aright till the sea itself floweth in your veins, till you are clothed with the heavens and crowned with the stars, and perceive yourself to be the sole heir of the whole world, and more than so because men are in it who are every one sole heirs as well as you. Till you can sing and rejoice and delight in God as misers do in gold and kings in sceptres you never enjoy the world.

30

Till your spirit filleth the whole world and the stars are your jewels; till you are as familiar with the ways of God in all ages as with your walk and table; till you are intimately acquainted with that shady nothing out of which the world was made; till you love men so as to desire their happiness with a thirst equal to the zeal of your own; till you delight in God for being good to all, you never enjoy the world. Till you more feel it than your private estate, and are more present in the hemisphere, considering the glories and the beauties there, than in your own house; till you remember how lately you were made, and how wonderful it was when you came into it, and more rejoice in the palace of your glory than if it had been made but today morning.

31

Yet further, you never enjoy the world aright till you so love the beauty of enjoying it that you are covetous and earnest to persuade others to enjoy it, and so perfectly hate the abominable corruption of men in despising it that you had rather suffer the flames of hell than willingly be guilty of their error. There is so much blindness and ingratitude and damned folly in it. The world is a mirror of infinite beauty, yet no man sees it. It is a temple of majesty yet no man regards it. It is a region of light and peace, did not men disquiet it. It is the paradise of God. It is more to man since he is fallen than it was before. It is the place of angels and the gate of heaven. When Jacob waked out of his dream he said, 'God is here and I wist it not. How dreadful is this place! This is none other than the house of God and the gate of heaven.'

40

Socrates was wont to say they are most happy and nearest the gods that needed nothing. And coming once up into the exchange at Athens where they that traded asked him, 'What will you buy? What do you lack?'—after he had gravely walked up into the middle, spreading forth his hands and turning about, 'Good gods,' saith he, 'who would have thought there were so many things in the world which I do not want!' And so left the place under the reproach of nature. He was wont to say that happiness consisted not in having many but in needing the fewest things; for the gods needed nothing at all, and they were most like them that least needed. We needed heaven and earth, our senses, such souls and such bodies, with infinite riches in the image of God to be enjoyed; which God of His mercy having freely prepared they are most happy that so live in the enjoyment of those as to need no accidental, trivial thing. No splendours, pomps and vanities. . . .

41

As pictures are made curious by lights and shades, which without shades could not be, so is felicity composed of wants and supplies, without which mixture there could be no felicity. Were there no needs wants would be wanting themselves, and supplies superfluous;

want being the parent of celestial treasure. It is very strange; want itself is a treasure in heaven, and so great an one, that without it there could be no treasure. God did infinitely for us when He made us to want like Gods, that like Gods we might be satisfied. The heathen deities wanted nothing and were therefore unhappy; for they had no being. But the Lord God of Israel, the living and true God, was from all eternity, and from all eternity wanted like a God. He wanted the communication of His divine essence, and persons to enjoy it. He wanted worlds, He wanted spectators, He wanted joys, He wanted treasures. He wanted, yet He wanted not, for He had them.

THE SECOND CENTURY

21

When Amasis the king of Egypt sent to the wise men of Greece, to know, 'Quid pulcherrimum' upon due and mature consideration they answered, 'The world'; the world certainly being so beautiful that nothing visible is capable of more. Were we to see it only once that first appearance would amaze us. But being daily seen we observe it not. Ancient philosophers have thought God to be the soul of the world. Since therefore this visible world is the body of God, not His natural body but which He hath assumed, let us see how glorious His wisdom is in manifesting Himself thereby. It hath not only represented His infinity and eternity which we thought impossible to be represented by a body, but His beauty also, His wisdom, goodness, power, life and glory, His righteousness, love and blessedness: all which as out of a plentiful treasury may be taken and collected out of this world.

First, His infinity; for the dimensions of the world are unsearchable. An infinite wall is a poor thing to express his infinity; a narrow, endless length is nothing;might be,and if it were,were unprofitable. But the world is round and endlessly unsearchable every way. What astronomer, what mathematician, what philosopher did ever comprehend the measures of the world? The very earth alone being round and globous is illimited. It hath neither walls, nor precipices, nor bounds, nor borders. A man may lose himself in the midst of nations and kingdoms. And yet it is but a centre compared to the universe. The distance of the sun, the altitude of the stars, the wideness of the heavens on every side passeth the reach of sight and search of the understanding; and whether it be infinite or no we cannot tell. The eternity of God is so apparent in it, that the wisest of philosophers thought the world eternal. We come into it and leave it as if it had neither beginning nor ending. Concerning its beauty I need say nothing. No man can turn unto it but must be ravished with its appearance: only thus much, since these things are so beautiful, how much more beautiful is the author of them. . . . But the beauty of God is invisible; it is all wisdom, goodness, life and love, power, glory, blessedness, etc. How therefore shall these be expressed in a material world? His wisdom is expressed in manifesting His infinity in such a commodious manner. He hath made a penetrable body in which we may stand, to wit the air, and see the heavens, and the regions of the earth at wonderful distances. His goodness is manifest in making that beauty so delightful and its varieties so profitable. The air to breathe in, the sea for moisture, the earth for fertility, the heavens for influences, the sun for productions, the stars and trees wherewith it is adorned for innumerable uses. Again His goodness is seen in the end to which He guideth all this profitableness, in making it serviceable to supply our wants and delight our senses; to enflame us with His love and make us amiable before Him, and delighters in His blessedness. God having not only showed us His simple infinity in an endless wall, but in such an illustrious manner, by an infinite variety, that He hath drowned our understanding in a multitude of wonders, transported us with delights, and enriched us with innumerable diversities of joys and pleasures. The very greatness of our felicity convinceth us that there is a God.

26

. . . For if God is love, and love be so restless a principle in exalting its object, and so secure that it always promoteth and glorifieth and exalteth itself thereby, where will there be any bounds in your exaltation? How dreadful, how amiable, how blessed, how great, how unsearchable, how incomprehensible must you be in your true, real, inward happiness. The object of love is infinitely exalted. Love is infinitely delightful to its object; God by all His works manifesteth Himself to be love, and you being the end of them are evidently its object. Go where you will, here alone shall you find your happiness. Contemplate therefore the works of God, for they serve you not only in manifesting Him but in making you to know yourself and your blessedness.

40

In all love there is a love begetting, a love begotten and a love proceeding. Which though they are one in essence subsist nevertheless in three several manners. For love is benevolent affection to another, which is of itself, and by itself relateth to its object. It floweth from itself and resteth in its object. Love proceedeth of necessity from itself, for unless it be of itself it is not love. Constraint is destructive and opposite to its nature. The love from which it floweth is the fountain of love; the love which streameth from it is the communication of love, or love communicated; and the love which resteth in the object is the love which streameth to it. So that in all love the trinity is clear. By secret passages without stirring it proceedeth to its object, and is as powerfully present as if it did not proceed at all, the love that lieth in the bosom of the lover being the love that is perceived in the spirit of the beloved; that is, the same in substance, though in the manner of substance or subsistence, different. Love in the bosom is the parent of love; love in the stream is the effect of love; love seen, or dwelling in the object, proceedeth from both. Yet are all three one and the self-same love, though three loves.

41

Love in the fountain and love in the stream are both the same. And therefore are they both equal in time and glory. For love communicateth itself, and therefore love in the fountain is the very love communicated to its object. Love in the fountain is love in the stream, and love in the stream equally glorious with love in the fountain. Though it streameth to its object it abideth in the lover, and is the love of the lover.

Where love is the lover, love streaming from the lover is the lover, the lover streaming from Himself and existing in another person.

This person is the Son of God, who as He is the wisdom of the Father so is He the love of the Father. For the love of the Father is the wisdom of the Father. And this person did God by loving us beget, that He might be the means of all our glory.

This person differs in nothing from the Father but only in this, that He is begotten of Him. He is eternal with the Father, as glorious and as intelligent. He is of the same mind in everything in all worlds, loveth the same objects in as infinite a measure. Is the means by which the Father loveth, acteth, createth, redeemeth, governeth and perfecteth all things. And the means also by which we see and love the Father, our strength and our eternity. He is the mediator between God and His creatures. God therefore being willing to redeem us by His own blood by Him redeemed us, and in His person died for us.

In all love there is some producer, some means and some end, all these being internal in the thing itself. Love loving is the producer, and that is the Father; love produced is the means, and that is the Son, for love is the means by which a lover loveth. The end of these means is love, for it is love by loving, and that is the Holy Ghost; the end and the producer being both the same by the means attained. For by loving love attaineth itself and being. The producer is attained by loving and is the end of Himself. That love is the end of itself, and that God loveth that He might be love, is as evident to him that considers spiritual things as the sun. Because it is impossible there should be a higher end or a better proposed. What can be more desirable than the most delightful operation; what more eligible than the most glorious being; what further can be proposed than the most blessed and perfect life? Since God therefore chooseth the most perfect life, what can be more perfect than that life and that being which is at once the fountain and the end of all things? There being in it the perpetual joy of giving and receiving infinite treasures. To be the fountain of joys and blessings is delightful, and by being love God is the fountain of all worlds. To receive all and be the end of all is equally delightful, and by being love God receiveth and is the end of all. For all the benefits that are done unto all, by loving all, Himself receiveth. What good could heaven and earth do Him, were it not for His love to the children of men? By being what He is, which is love unto all, He enjoyeth all.

47

What life can be more pleasant than that which is delighted in itself and in all objects, in which also all objects infinitely delight? What life can be more pleasant than that which is blessed in all and glorious before all? Now this life is the life of love. For this end therefore did He desire to love that He might be love; infinitely delightful to all objects, infinitely delighted in all, and infinitely pleased in Himself for being delightful to all, and delighted in all. All this He attaineth by love. For love is the most delightful of all employments; all the objects of love are delightful to it, and love is delightful to all its objects. Well then may love be the end of loving, which is so complete; it being a thing so delightful that God infinitely rejoiceth in Himself for being love. And thus you see how God is the end of Himself. He doth what He doth that He may be what He is: wise and glorious and bountiful and blessed in being perfect love.

48

Love is so divine and perfect a thing that it is worthy to be the very end and being of the Deity. It is His goodness, and it is His glory. We therefore so vastly delight in love because all these excellencies and all other whatsoever lie within it. By loving a soul does propagate and beget itself. By loving it does dilate and magnify itself. By loving it does enlarge and delight itself. By loving also it delighteth others, as by loving it doth honour and enrich itself. But above all, by loving it does attain itself, love also being the end of souls, which are never perfect till they are in act what they are in power. They were made to love and are dark and vain and comfortless till they do it. Till they love they are idle or misemployed. Till they love they are desolate, without their objects, and narrow and little and dishonourable: but when they shine by love upon all objects they are accompanied with them and enlightened by them. Till we become therefore all act as God is, we can never rest, nor ever be satisfied.

51

Love is a far more glorious being than flesh and bones. If thou wilt, it is endless and infinitely more sweet than thy body can be to thee and others. Thy body is confined, and is a dull lump of heavy clay by which thou art retarded rather than dost move. It was given thee to be a lantern only to the candle of love that shineth in thy soul. By it thou dost see and feel and eat and drink, but the end of all is that thou mightest be as God is, a joy and blessing by being love. Thy love is illimited. Thy love can extend to all objects. Thy love can see God and accompany His love throughout all eternity. Thy love is infinitely profitable to thyself and others; to thyself for thereby mayest thou receive infinite good things, to others for thereby thou art prone to do infinite good to all. Thy body can receive but few pleasures; thy love can feed upon all, take into itself all worlds, and all eternities above all worlds and all the joys of God before and after. Thy flesh and bones can do but little good, nor that little unless as by love it is inspired and directed. A poor carcass thy body is, but love is delightful and profitable to thousands. O live therefore by the more noble part. Be like Him who baptizeth with fire; feel thy spirit, awaken thy soul, be an enlarged seraphim, an infinite good, or like unto Him.

54

Love is infinitely delightful to its object, and the more violent the more glorious. It is infinitely high, nothing can hurt it, and infinitely great in all extremes of beauty and excellence. Excess is its true moderation, activity its rest and burning fervency its only refreshment. Nothing is more glorious yet nothing more humble; nothing more precious yet nothing more cheap; nothing more familiar yet nothing so inaccessible; nothing more nice yet nothing more laborious; nothing more liberal yet nothing more covetous. It doth all things for its object's sake, yet it is the most self-ended thing in the whole world, for of all things in nature it can least endure to be displeased. Since therefore it containeth so many miracles it may well contain this one more, that it maketh everyone greatest, and among lovers everyone is supreme and sovereign.

65

You are as prone to love as the sun is to shine, it being the most delightful and natural employment of the soul of man, without which you are dark and miserable. Consider therefore the extent of love, its vigour and excellency. For certainly he that delights not in love makes vain the universe, and is of necessity to himself the greatest burden. The whole world ministers to you as the theatre of your love. It sustains you and all objects that you may continue to love them, without which it were better for you to have no being. Life without objects is sensible emptiness. Objects without love are the delusion of life. The objects of love are its greatest treasures, and without love it is impossible they should be treasures. For the objects which we love are the pleasing objects, and delightful things. And whatsoever is not pleasing and delightful to us can be no treasure. Nay, it is distasteful, and worse than nothing, since we had rather it should have no being.

66

That violence wherewith sometimes a man doteth upon one creature is but a little spark of that love, even towards all, which lurketh in his nature. We are made to love, both to satisfy the necessity of our active nature and to answer the beauties in every creature. By love our souls are married and soldered to the creatures, and it is our duty like God to be united to them all. We must love them infinitely, but in God and for God, and God in them, namely all His excellencies manifested in them. When we dote upon the perfections and beauties of some one creature we do not love that too much but other things too little. Never was anything in this world loved too much; but many things have been loved in a false way, and all in too short a measure.

This visible world is wonderfully to be delighted in and highly to be esteemed because it is the theatre of God's righteous kingdom, who as Himself was righteous because He made it freely, so He made it that we might freely be righteous too. For in the kingdom of glory it is impossible to fall. No man can sin that clearly seeth the beauty of God's face, because no man can sin against his own happiness. That is, none can when he sees it clearly willingly and wittingly forsake it. Tempter, temptation, loss and danger being all seen, but here we see His face in a glass, and more dimly behold our happiness as in a mirror. By faith therefore we are to live and to sharpen our eye that we may see His glory. We are to be studious and intent in our desires and endeavours, for we may sin or we may be holy. Holiness therefore and righteousness naturally flow out of our fruition of the world. For who can vilify and debase himself by any sin while he actually considers he is the heir of it? It exalts a man to a sublime and honourable life; it lifts him above lusts and makes him angelical.

THE THIRD CENTURY

1

Will you see the infancy of this sublime and celestial greatness? Those pure and virgin apprehensions I had from the womb, and that divine light wherewith I was born are the best unto this day wherein I can see the universe. By the gift of God they attended me into the world, and by His special favour I remember them till now. Verily they seem the greatest gifts His wisdom could bestow, for without them all other gifts had been dead and vain. They are unattainable by book, and therefore I will teach them by experience. Pray for them earnestly, for they will make you angelical and wholly celestial. Certainly Adam in paradise had not more sweet and curious apprehensions of the world than I when I was a child.

2

All appeared new and strange at the first, inexpressibly rare and delightful and beautiful. I was a little stranger which at my entrance into the world was saluted and surrounded with innumerable joys. My knowledge was divine: I knew by intuition those things which since my apostasy I collected again by the highest reason. My very ignorance was advantageous. I seemed as one brought into the estate of innocence. All things were spotless and pure and glorious; yea, and infinitely mine, and joyful and precious. I knew not that there were any sins or complaints or laws. I dreamed not of poverties, contentions or vices. All tears and quarrels were hidden from mine eyes. Everything was at rest, free, and immortal. I knew nothing of sickness or death or exaction; in the absence of these I was entertained like an angel with the works of God in their splendour and glory. I saw all in the peace of Eden; heaven and earth did sing my Creator's praises, and could not make more melody to Adam than to me. All time was eternity and a perpetual sabbath. Is it not strange that an infant should be heir of the world, and see those mysteries which the books of the learned never unfold?

3

The corn was orient and immortal wheat, which never should be reaped nor was ever sown. I thought it had stood from everlasting to everlasting. The dust and stones of the street were as precious as gold. The gates were at first the end of the world; the green trees when I saw them first through one of the gates transported and ravished me; their sweetness and unusual beauty made my heart to leap, and almost mad with ecstasy, they were such strange and wonderful things. The men! O what venerable and reverend creatures did the aged seem! Immortal cherubims! And young men glittering and sparkling angels, and maids strange seraphic pieces of life and beauty! Boys and girls tumbling in the street and playing were moving jewels. I knew not that they were born or should die. But all things abided eternally as they were in their proper places. Eternity was manifest in the light of the day, and something infinite behind everything appeared, which talked with my expectation and moved my desire. The city seemed to stand in Eden, or to be built in heaven. The streets were mine, the temple was mine, the people were mine, their clothes and gold and silver was mine as much as their sparkling eyes, fair skins and ruddy faces. The skies were mine and so were the sun and moon and stars, and all the world was mine and I the only spectator and enjoyer of it. I knew no churlish proprieties, nor bounds, nor divisions; but all proprieties and divisions were mine, all treasures and the possessors of them. So that with much ado I was corrupted, and made to learn the dirty devices of this world. Which now I unlearn, and become as it were a little child again, that I may enter into the kingdom of God.

5

Our Saviour's meaning when He said, 'He must be born again and become a little child that will enter into the kingdom of heaven' is deeper far than is generally believed. It is not only in a careless reliance upon divine providence that we are to become little children, or in the feebleness and shortness of our anger and simplicity of our passions; but in the peace and purity of all our soul. Which purity also is a deeper thing than is commonly apprehended; for we must disrobe ourselves of all false colours, and unclothe our souls of evil habits; all our thoughts must be infant-like and clear, the powers of our soul free from the leaven of this world, and disentangled from men's conceits and customs. Grit in the eye or the yellow jaundice will not let a man see those objects truly that are before it. And therefore it is requisite that we should be as very strangers to the thoughts, customs and opinions of men in this world, as if we were but little children. So those things would appear to us only which do to children when they are first born. Ambitions, trades, luxuries, inordinate affections, casual and accidental riches invented since the fall would be gone, and only those things appear which did to Adam in paradise, in the same light and in the same colours: God in His works, glory in the light, love in our parents, men, ourselves, and the face of heaven. Every man naturally seeing those things to the enjoyment of which he is naturally born.

6

Everyone provideth objects but few prepare senses whereby, and light wherein, to see them. Since therefore we are born to be a burning and shining light and whatever men learn of others they see in the light of others' souls, I will in the light of my soul show you the universe. Perhaps it is celestial and will teach you how beneficial we may be to each other. I am sure it is a sweet and curious light to me, which had I wanted I would have given all the gold and silver in all worlds to have purchased. But it was the gift of God and could not be bought with money. And by what steps and degrees I proceeded to that enjoyment of all eternity which now I possess I will likewise show you. A clear and familiar light it may prove unto you.

7

The first light which shined in my infancy in its primitive and inno-cent clarity was totally eclipsed, insomuch that I was fain to learn all again. If you ask me how it was eclipsed, truly by the customs and manners of men, which like contrary winds blew it out; by an innumerable company of other objects, rude, vulgar and worthless things that like so many loads of earth and dung did overwhelm and bury it; by the impetuous torrent of wrong desires in all others whom I saw or knew that carried me away and alienated me from it: by a whole sea of other matters and concernments that covered and drowned it; finally by the evil influence of a bad education that did not foster and cherish it. All men's thoughts and words were about other matters; they all prized new things which I did not dream of. I was a stranger and unacquainted with them; I was little and reverenced their authority; I was weak, and easily guided by their example; ambitious also, and desirous to approve myself unto them. And finding no one syllable in any man's mouth of those things, by degrees they vanished; my thoughts (as indeed what is more fleeting than a thought) were blotted out. And at last all the celestial, great and stable treasures to which I was born, as wholly forgotten, as if they had never been.

8

Had any man spoken of it, it had been the most easy thing in the world to have taught me and to have made me believe that heaven and earth was God's house, and that He gave it me; that the sun was mine, and that men were mine, and that cities and kingdoms were mine also; that earth was better than gold and that water was, every drop of it, a precious jewel. And that these were great and living treasures, and that all riches whatsoever else was dross in comparison. From whence I clearly find how docible our nature is in natural things, were it rightly entreated, and that our misery proceedeth ten thousand times more from the outward bondage of opinion and custom than from any inward corruption or depravity of nature; and that it is not our parents' loins as much as our parents' lives that enthrals and blinds us. Yet is all our corruption derived from Adam, inasmuch as all the evil examples and inclinations of the world arise from his sin. But I speak it in the presence of God and of our lord Jesus Christ, in my pure, primitive, virgin light, while my apprehensions were natural and unmixed, I cannot remember but that I was ten thousand times more prone to good and excellent things than evil. But I was quickly tainted and fell by others.

9

It was a difficult matter to persuade me that the tinselled ware upon a hobby-horse was a fine thing. They did impose upon me, and obtrude their gifts, that made me believe a ribbon or a feather curious. I could not see where the curiousness or fineness; and to teach me that a purse of gold was of any value seemed impossible, the art by which it becomes so and the reasons for which it is accounted so were so deep and hidden to my inexperience. So that nature is still nearest to natural things and farthest off from preternatural, and to esteem that the reproach of nature is an error in them only who are unacquainted with it. Natural things are glorious, and to know them glorious; but to call things preternatural natural, monstrous. Yet all they do it, who esteem gold, silver, houses, lands, clothes etc. the riches of nature, which are indeed the riches of invention. Nature knows no such riches but art and error makes them. Not the God of nature but sin only was the parent of them. The riches of nature are our souls and bodies, with all their faculties, senses and endowments. And it had been the easiest thing in the whole world, that all felicity consisted in the enjoyment of all the world, that it was prepared for me before I was born, and that nothing was more divine and beautiful.

10

Thoughts are the most present things to thoughts, and of the most powerful influence. My soul was only apt and disposed to great things; but souls to souls are like apples to apples, one being rotten rots another. When I began to speak and go nothing began to be present to me but was present in their thoughts. Nor was anything present to me any other way than it was so to them. The glass of imagination was the only mirror wherein anything was represented or appeared to me. All things were absent which they talked not of. So I began among my playfellows to prize a drum, a fine coat, a penny, a gilded book etc., who before never dreamed of any such wealth; goodly objects to drown all the knowledge of heaven and earth. As for the heavens and the sun and stars they disappeared, and were no more unto me than the bare walls. So that the strange riches of man's invention quite overcame the riches of nature, being learned more laboriously and in the second place.

12

By this you may see who are the rude and barbarous Indians. For verily there is no savage nation under the cope of heaven that is more absurdly barbarous than the Christian world. They that go naked and drink water and live upon roots are like Adam, or angels in comparison of us. But they indeed that call beads and glass buttons jewels and dress themselves with feather, and buy pieces of brass and broken hafts of knives of our merchants are somewhat like us. But we pass them in barbarous opinions and monstrous apprehensions, which we nickname civility and the mode amongst us. I am sure those barbarous people that go naked come nearer to Adam, God and angels, in the simplicity of their wealth though not in knowledge.

14

Being swallowed up therefore in the miserable gulf of idle talk and worthless vanities thenceforth I lived among shadows, like a prodigal son feeding upon husks with swine. A comfortless wilderness full of thorns and troubles the world was; or worse, a waste place covered with idleness and play and shops and markets and taverns. As for churches they were things I did not understand. And schools were a burden, so that there was nothing in the world worth the having or enjoying but my game and sport, which also was a dream and being past wholly forgotten. So that I had utterly forgotten all goodness, bounty, comfort and glory, which things are the very brightness of the glory of God; for lack of which therefore He was unknown.

15

Yet sometimes in the midst of these dreams I should come a little to myself, so far as to feel I wanted something, secretly to expostulate with God for not giving me riches, to long after an unknown happiness, to grieve that the world was so empty, and to be dissatisfied with my present state because it was vain and forlorn. I had heard of angels, and much admired that here upon earth nothing should be but dirt and streets and gutters; for as for the pleasures that were in great men's houses I had not seen them, and it was my real happiness they were unknown, for because nothing deluded me I was the more inquisitive.

16

Once I remember (I think I was about four years old) when I thus reasoned with myself, sitting in a little obscure room in my father's poor house. If there be a God certainly He must be infinite in goodness. And that I was prompted to by a real whispering instinct of nature. And if He be infinite in goodness and a perfect Being in wisdom and love, certainly He must do most glorious things, and give us infinite riches. How comes it to pass therefore that I am so poor, of so scanty and narrow a fortune, enjoying few and obscure comforts? I thought I could not believe Him a God to me unless all His power were employed to glorify me. I knew not then my soul or body, nor did I think of the heavens and the earth, the rivers and the stars, the sun or the seas; all those were lost and absent from me. But when I found them made out of nothing for me, then I had a God indeed, whom I could praise and rejoice in.

17

Sometimes I should be alone and without employment, when suddenly my soul would return to itself and forgetting all things in the whole world which mine eyes had seen would be carried away to the ends of the earth. And my thoughts would be deeply engaged with enquiries: how the earth did end, whether walls did bound it, or sudden precipices, or whether the heavens by degrees did come to touch it, so that the face of the earth and heaven were so near that a man with difficulty could creep under? Whatever I could imagine was inconvenient, and my reason being posed was quickly wearied. What also upheld the earth (because it was heavy) and kept it from falling, whether pillars or dark waters? And if any of these what then upheld those, and what again those, of which I saw there would be no end. Little did I think that the earth was round, and the world so full of beauty, light and wisdom. When I saw that, I knew by the perfection of the work there was a God, and was satisfied and rejoiced. People underneath and fields and flowers with another sun and another day pleased me mightily, but more when I knew it was the same sun that served them by night that served us by day.

22

. . . I remember once, the first time I came into a magnificent or noble dining-room and was left there alone, I rejoiced to see the gold and state and carved imagery. But when all was dead and there was no motion I was weary of it and departed dissatisfied. But afterwards, when I saw it full of lords and ladies and music and dancing the place which once seemed not to differ from a solitary den had now entertainment and nothing of tediousness, but pleasure in it. By which I perceived (upon a reflection made long after) that men and women are when well understood a principal part of our true felicity. By this I found also that nothing that stood still could by doing so be a part of happiness, and that affection, though it were invisible, was the best of motions. But the august and glorious exercise of virtue was more solemn and divine which yet I saw not. And that all men and angels should appear in heaven.

23

Another time, in a lowering and sad evening, being alone in the field, when all things were dead and quiet, a certain want and horror fell upon me, beyond imagination. The unprofitableness and silence of the place dissatisfied me, its wideness terrified me, from the utmost ends of the earth fears surrounded me. How did I know but dangers might suddenly arise from the east, and invade me from the unknown regions beyond the seas? I was a weak and little child, and had forgotten there was a man alive in the earth. Yet something also of hope and expectation comforted me from every border. This taught me that I was concerned in all the world, and that in the remotest borders the causes of peace delight me; and the beauties of the earth when seen were made to entertain me; that I was made to hold a communion with the secrets of divine providence in all the world; that a remembrance of all the joys I had from my birth ought always to be with me; that the presence of cities, temples and kingdoms ought to sustain me; and that to be alone in the world was to be desolate and miserable. The comfort of houses and friends, and the clear assurance of treasures everywhere, God's care and love, His goodness, wisdom and power, His presence and watchfulness in all the ends of the earth were my strength and assurance forever; and that these things being absent to my eye were my joys and consolations, as present to my understanding as the wideness and emptiness of the universe which I saw before me.

46

When I came into the country, and being seated among silent trees, had all my time in mine own hands, I resolved to spend it all, whatever it cost me, in search of happiness, and to satiate that burning thirst which nature had enkindled in me from my youth. In which I was so resolute that I chose rather to live upon £10 a year and to go in leather clothes and feed upon bread and water, so that I might have all my time clearly to myself, than to keep many thousands per annum in an estate of life where my time would be devoured in care and labour. And God was so pleased to accept of that desire that from that time to this I have had all things plentifully provided for me, without any care at all, my very study of felicity making me more to prosper than all the care in the whole world. So that through His blessing I live a free and kingly life, as if the world were turned again into Eden, or much more, as it is at this day.

And what rule do you think I walked by? Truly a strange one, but the best in the whole world. I was guided by an implicit faith in God's goodness, and therefore led to the study of the most obvious and common things. For thus I thought within myself: God being, as we generally believe, infinite in goodness, it is most consonant and agreeable with His nature that the best things should be most common. For nothing is more natural to infinite goodness than to make the best things most frequent, and only things worthless scarce. Then I began to enquire what things were most common: air, light, heaven and earth, water, the sun, trees, men and women, cities, temples, etc. These I found common and obvious to all. Rubies, pearls, diamonds, gold and silver, these I found scarce and to the most denied. Then began I to consider and compare the value of them, which I measured by their serviceableness, and by the excellencies which would be found in them should they be taken away. And in conclusion I saw clearly that there was a real valuableness in all the common things; in the scarce, a feigned.